Silvertown Life

A Boy's Story

by
Stan Dyson

AuthorHouse™ UK Ltd.
500 Avebury Boulevard
Central Milton Keynes, MK9 2BE
www.authorhouse.co.uk
Phone: 08001974150

This book is a work of non-fiction. Unless otherwise noted, the author and the publisher make no explicit guarantees as to the accuracy of the information contained in this book and in some cases, names of people and places have been altered to protect their privacy.

© 2008 Stan Dyson. All rights reserved.

No part of this book may be reproduced, stored in a retrieval system, or transmitted by any means without the written permission of the author.

First published by AuthorHouse 7/3/2008

ISBN: 978-1-4343-9088-2 (sc)
ISBN: 978-1-4343-9089-9 (hc)

Printed in the United States of America
Bloomington, Indiana

This book is printed on acid-free paper.

I am grateful to Newham Archives and Local Studies Library for their kind permission to use those of the pictures in this book, which are their copyright.

Front Cover photo Glen Pattison, George Beautyman, Henry Taylor, Terry Beautyman & Stan Dyson Taken in Westwood Road, West Silvertown 1958

This book is dedicated to my Grandchildren, Reece, Ellis, Chloe & Davis Pearce

Into my heart an air that kills
    From yon far country blows:
  What are those blue remembered hills?
  What spires, what farms are those?

  That is the land of lost content,
    I see it shining plain,
  Those happy highways where I went
    And cannot come again.

Alfred Edward Houseman

1

The Early Years

I was born at Forest Gate Hospital, London, at around 10.30 pm on Saturday 27th January 1945, and just months away from the end of the Second World War. My mother's name was Catherine Ellen Dyson (nee Guinee) and she was always called Kath and my father's name was Alfred Stanley Dyson and he was always called Stan. Dad spent virtually his whole working life as a maintenance engineer for Tate & Lyle sugar importers at the Thames Refinery in Silvertown, opposite Silvertown Railway Station where, for some inexplicable reason, all his work mates all called him 'George'. He served with British forces in Germany during the Second World War in the Royal Electrical & Mechanical Engineers. Prior to fighting in France and Germany he was working at Thames Refinery at the very start of 'The Blitz' on the night of 7th September 1940 when Silvertown and North Woolwich Docklands came under the first intense German aerial bombardment from 550 German aircraft. The Silvertown Dockland area was extensively damaged by high explosives and was ablaze. I still have Dad's commendation letter dated 10th September 1940 that he received from Tate & Lyle Director, Peter Runge, part of which states 'The calmness shown under intensive bombardment sets an example of bravery which will not be surpassed.'

Mum and Dad got married on Christmas Day 1943, with Dad in his full army uniform.

We lived at number eleven Westwood Road, West Silvertown, adjacent to the Victoria Docks, with the Jubilee Public House at the North Woolwich Road end of our road and the old chapel, later in the mid fifties a café, on the corner opposite. The back entrance of the St Barnabus Church and the main entrance to the church hall were situated at the Evelyn Road docks end of Westwood Road, directly opposite the entrance to West Silvertown Primary School. The houses opposite our house were bombed wrecks. They were destroyed by the very first wave of German bombers on 7th September 1940, the very moment Dad was fighting the factory fires under bombardment at Tate & Lyle Thames Refinery at the other end of Silvertown. That huge explosion between Westwood Road and Hanameel Street blew out the front doors and windows of most of the houses opposite. Mum was single and living with Nan at number fifteen Westwood Road at the time of the explosion. She often told me the story of how she was in the passageway at the point of impact and detonation of the bomb and that in the subsequent explosion she was blown the whole length of the house right into the scullery. She said that she thought that it was her lot!

The West Silvertown hamlet was made up of thirteen roads of Victorian terraced houses, originally built in the early 1880's for the Dockworkers and local industry employees, running alongside the Royal Victoria Docks from Clyde Road and Ellesmere Road to Mill Road. Clyde Road and Ellesmere Road were opposite Tate & Lyle (Plaistow Wharf) and Mill Road was just about opposite Crescent Wharf, where the great Silvertown Explosion took place at Brunner Monds TNT factory on Friday 19th January 1917. Both Clyde and Ellesmere Roads were completely destroyed by bombs in the Second World War.

Most of the terraced houses had three rooms upstairs, three more downstairs and outside in the yard, a lavatory. They were fairly dismal dwellings on the inside. Most of the houses had the interior woodwork painted either dark brown or dark green and the walls were covered in distemper, in some cases with random splodges of a different colour emulsion paint scattered across the walls just to break the monotony.

Silvertown Life

Stan with his mother Catherine 1946

All rooms had a real coal fireplace, although it was customary just to have the fire in the main living rooms, unless it was a particularly cold winter when you could be treated with a real coal fire in the bedroom. In our house only the front room and middle dining room had a square of carpet on the floor, generally laid over the top of the hardwearing linoleum floor covering material. The other three bedrooms and scullery were also laid with the linoleum. As we got into the 1950's dad upgraded the downstairs wall decoration in the front room and dining room with hardwearing dark brown 'lincrusta' type of wall paper on the bottom half of the wall with a lighter shade patterned wall paper on the top half of the wall and a two inch wide strip of border wallpaper covering the halfway area where the two wallpapers were joined together. The rest of the rooms in the house remained distempered.

During the winter months the 'Coalman' would call each week and, carrying one hundred weight sacks of coal across his hunched forward shoulders and back, he would walk down the passageway into the very centre of our house and then discharge the complete load of coal and coal dust into the cupboard under the stairs. There was a thunderous roar as he tipped the load forward into the cupboard and it crashed onto the wooden floorboards. From the age of about 5-years onwards I was honoured to have the job of quickly slamming the under-stairs cupboard door the very moment the coalman turned to collect the second hundredweight sack-load of coal. This action was supposed to minimise the resultant cloud of coal dust that erupted from the under-stairs cupboard and cascaded down the long narrow passageway between the street door and the scullery. I was also given the job of sweeping all the coal dust from the linoleum-covered passageway afterwards. After completion of the task I then looked just like a miniature coalman, covered in the coal dust and subsequently had to endure a good scrubbing down in the tin bath that had always hung on the wall in the outside back yard. There were no internal hot water taps in those days, just a solitary brass cold water tap attached to a lead pipe, so after the tin bath was just half full of freezing cold water mum would then pour in a couple of kettles of boiling hot water, straight off the oven gas ring. This only just took the chill off the icy water and then my 'scrubbing down' ordeal in our draughty scullery began – I never really looked forward to the weekly winter coal delivery day.

It was bitterly cold in those Victorian terraced houses during the winter months, especially as due to the fact that most families were relatively poor, therefore only one fire, or possibly two fires in very cold weather, were kept burning during the daytime hours. Ice would form on the insides of the windows! First thing early each morning was the ritual fire lighting exercise. After a period of training from dad I was then allowed to actually light the fire right from scratch. This was almost a survival skill; firstly removing the front page of yesterday's newspaper and then tearing all the other pages into two halves, then screwing up each part into a small ball and placing them into the fire-grate. When the area of the fire-grate was completely covered I would then pull the rubber band off the bundle of wood and then carefully lay some of the thin sticks in a criss-cross pattern across the crumpled newspaper pieces. I would continue by laying individual small pieces of coal across the wood, taking care to only cover about half the total area so that you could still see both the firewood and the newspaper underneath. Then I would selectively start lighting the newspaper in several areas at the front and then as this area started to burn I would drop a couple of lighted matches into the middle. I would carefully watch the wood and when I was sure that the wood had really caught fire, I would at this point load on more coal, and then I would pick up the discarded first double-pages of the newspaper and hold it right across the entire front of the fire-grate, leaving a six-inch gap at the bottom. This would cause an accelerated draft to pass through the gap causing the fire to roar away underneath the newspaper cover and make the wood burn fiercely to ignite the coal. You had to very carefully watch the slight orange glow of the fire through the newspaper until it turned a fiery red and was really roaring away. This was a critical point, because if you did not whip the paper away at the right moment it could also catch fire and become a hazard. In those days fire lighting was a real mans skill that was taught from father to son. Mum was really quite useless at lighting the fire, invariably the coal failed to ignite, then you had lost both yesterday's newspaper and a valuable quantity of firewood.

We shared our house with the Batterbee family. They lived in the three rooms upstairs and we had the scullery, middle living room and front bedroom downstairs. Until 1944 Ted and Bridgette Batterbee had lived at 31 Evelyn Road, but German bombing had destroyed their house, subsequently they knocked on our door seeking shelter and mum took them into our house. This was a common practice for families whose houses were destroyed by bombs and in keeping with the camaraderie that existed in the West Silvertown hamlet. Bombed out families would walk around the streets just asking other householders if they had sufficient room to take them in. As dad was away fighting the Germans in WW2 there was only mum occupying the six rooms in our house, so she just invited them in. I do not believe dad was too pleased on his return from Germany at the end of November 1946 to find the top part of his house occupied by another family.

Silvertown was a real hive of industry, being situated between the Royal Docks and the River Thames. Most of the major employers had their factories running from West Silvertown to North Woolwich, British Oil & Cake Mills, Pinchin Johnsons, Tate and Lyle Plaistow Wharf, John Knights, Venestas, Gulf Oil, Silcocks, Hollis Bros Timber

Stan Dyson

Merchants, Silvertown Tarmacadum Company, Spencer Chapman, Dicks Asbestos, Thomas W Ward, Silvertown Rubber Company, Keillers, Tate & Lyle Thames Refinery, Loders & Nucoline, Standard Telephones and Cables, Henleys Cables, and of course both Ranks & Spillers Flour Mills situated within the Royal Docks. With the exception of the Flour Mills and Hollis Timber, that backed onto the Royal Docks, all of these industries backed onto the River Thames and had jetties and cranes to load and unload goods onto the boats.

Lyle Park, situated in Bradfield Road, was the prominent leisure feature in West Silvertown and a great meeting place for all us kids. Abraham Lyle opened it in July 1924 for the benefit and recreation of West Silvertown residents. It had swings, a slide and a see-saw in the children's play area and a tennis court, putting green and a large central grassed area used for football and cricket by the adults. The end of the park was a raised area containing a Bandstand, sheltered seating within a hut and various open-air seats directly overlooking the Thames. One of my earliest living terrifying memories was of being in Lyle Park. I must have been just over one-year of age and could not yet speak, or probably walk, but funny enough I could understand quite a lot that was said to me. The reason I recall this with such clarity is because it coincided with a very traumatic event for me. An event that, due to lack of speech, I could not explain to my mother. A girl, I would now guess to be about 12-years of age, knocked at our house and ask my mother if she could take me out in my pushchair to Lyle Park. Judging by the look on her face mum was probably delighted to have the opportunity of the break. When we arrived in Lyle Park the girl went to the prickly holly bush that grew in abundance alongside the large hut opposite the War Memorial fountain, and picked off some of the rigid spiked leaves. She then wheeled me into the ladies toilets and proceeded to torture me by digging the spiked holly leaves into various parts of my body and face. The second time she called at our house for me I screamed and cried, probably in the hope that mum would say no, but no such luck. I remember looking back at mum, crying, as the girl wheeled the pushchair away from the house and mum shouting to the girl, "He'll be alright once he's out."

On this second visit to the park, the girl again plucked the holly leaves and took me into the ladies toilets. I was terrified. The torture commenced immediately, by the girl sticking the sharp point of the holly leaf into my legs. I was screaming and she then shouted, "Stop it, or I'll poke one right into your eyes!" I remember closing my eyes tightly, in fear, and the girl saying, "Right, it's your eyes now." I waited for the pain, but there was a softer sensation as something pressed against my tightly closed eye. The girl then said, "Silly, open your eyes and look; it's just a paint brush." I opened my eyes and recall seeing her laughing and holding a small paintbrush. I was really distressed and can still vividly recall the multicoloured paintbrush looking for all the world as if it were part of a 1970's discotheque psychedelic wall projection image. When she took me back home and mum saw how distressed I was she must have at that stage realised something was wrong, because that was an end of my Lyle Park torture trips. We had an addition to our family on 1st January 1948 when my sister Kathleen was born, although I cannot recall very much about the early years with my sister.

Another slightly less stressful early-memory was being dragged to my first day at school on 13th September 1949. West Silvertown Primary School was a huge complex that was, from the 1940's onwards, vastly under used. Only one third of it was used for teaching purposes, being under half of the central area bordering Boxley Street. Over half the complex, bordering the Westwood Road side was used by a commercial organisation to store large pallets and huge wooden boxes. The other unused part of the school was the annex on the right hand side of the school as you entered from the Westwood Road side. The only time it was opened was lunchtime for the preparation and service of school dinners. Stored in the large area immediately alongside this annex was a huge mountain of coke that was used to stoke the open fires in each classroom during the winter months. This massive 'coke mountain' was a real magnet for us kids to climb over in later years, whilst playing 'Cowboys and Indians' or 'Cops and Robbers'. We all inevitably ended up as black as the coalmen who delivered it and we suffered by enduring a cold scrub up in the tin baths in our draughty sculleries afterwards.

Although initially distressed, along with many others, at being thrust into the school environment I really enjoyed my first year at primary school. I would attribute this to the wonderful Miss Peacock, my first teacher. She was such a kind and understanding person and always with a radiant and beaming smile. I would estimate that in 1949 she must have been around forty-five years of age. She was full of energy and enthusiasm and despite being a 'Miss' she clearly loved children and had found her true vocation. She was about 5ft 6ins height, thin and with hair bordering ginger and always wore a floral, pastel, type of smock. An almost every day part of the first year ritual was to play with the small trays of fine sand and sea shells, probably the very same items my mum played with when she sat in this very classroom in 1920. We also played with plasticine and beanbags and played lots of games, like Oranges and Lemons, Ring a Ring O' Roses and 'The Big Ship Sails through the Alley, Alley Oh.' Also there was a large wooden swing in the classroom, and a Wendy House for the girls. Initially I sat next to a girl who lived in Bradfield Road called Wendy Bigwood, but after an incident that occurred between us her mother complained and I was moved next to Gloria Woolf who's family ran the café and bakers shop on the corner of Cranbrook Road.

I have some limited memories of the 1951 Festival of Britain. I remember my Aunt Alice, dad's sister, bringing me back from a trip to relatives in Portsmouth and after leaving the train we had to cross one of the London bridges. It was late evening and I remember looking from the bridge to the South Bank Exhibition and seeing the Skylon looking every bit like a giant javelin that had just dropped from the sky and stopped, frozen just before impact in the ground. Everything was lit up and I was fascinated by it all. Because of my excitement Dad took me to the South Bank Exhibition. I was delighted with all the exhibits inside the Dome of Discovery and I was absolutely amazed with the Skylon, seemingly just hanging suspended in mid-air. I saw how sticks of sweet rock were made and at the Silvertown Festival of Britain party all the floats paraded round the streets ending up in Lyle Park.

I also have very fond memories of the June 1953 Queen Elizabeth 2nd Coronation. I was part of the Westwood Road 'Cowboys and Indians' float. Mum had to cover me in a mixture of cocoa and water, as I was one of the Indians. When she took me to join the others, on the back of the Tate & Lyle open back lorry one of the other mothers said "He's far too light for an Indian Cathy, you haven't put enough cocoa on him." I was dragged back home and a much thicker paste was applied. I can still smell it today! All us 'Westwood Road' kids sat on the back of the lorry, around the tepee, and joined all the other floats on the winding journey around all the West Silvertown streets, finishing in Lyle Park. It was a great day in Lyle Park and all us kids were given a small toy. I recall that mine was a 'Dinky' toy lorry. We all had a huge party in West Silvertown Primary School hall and we also had a fancy dress competition. This must all have taken place over a weekend, because what with dressing up as Cowboys and Indians, having a fancy dress competition and normal everyday dress at the party it could not have possibly fitted into just one day. All us kid's were given a commemorative Coronation Biro pen and pencil set.

I was dressed as a Pirate for the fancy dress competition. To add to the authenticity I was made to wear a pirate facemask. It was nothing too elaborate, as the event coincided with the time that Kellogs Cornflakes boxes had cutout masks on the back and clearly someone thought that it would be a good idea to just cut out and attach the pirate mask monstrosity to my face. I just wish that they had ensured that it was removed at the time the official photograph was taken. It really did spoil the group photo for me, because it meant that my face was missing from the photograph of that historic event. Everyone who retained the photo must wonder who was the idiot in that mask. Tommy Batterbee won the boy's event, dressed as Al Jolson, but I can't recall who won the girl's event. The only other boy with his face partially covered was Jimmy Carrott, dressed as a Medieval Knight, with his visor down. I remember that he got a good clump from his Mum, Violet, for getting absolutely nowhere in the competition. There was no hanging around, or waiting until he got outside, it was 'whack', take that in front of all and sundry. I do believe that the Batterbee's, who you will recall lived upstairs, had a lot of input in the creation of both me, and my Sister Kathy's, fancy dress outfits.

One traumatic event happened around this period. Tommy Batterbee, who was my age, could not cut a loaf of bread. In our house we did not have the luxury of a cut loaf in those days, it was all full baked crusty loaves, and as no one other than him and me were in the house Tommy brought his loaf downstairs for me to cut, as I was more skilled than Tommy in using the large sharp bread knife. While I was cutting through the loaf Tommy saw a box of matches on our sideboard. He opened them and to my horror started to strike them and throw them around our living room. I was horrified, because I had nightmares about fires and shouted for him to stop. He didn't stop, but started striking two and three matches together and throwing them across the room. In a panic I grabbed one in mid air and it burnt me. I can't remember what happened after that – it's as if my mind has just blotted it out. I remember running up Westwood Road and turning right at the Jubilee Pub running as fast as I could into Mrs Pattison's Greengrocery shop shouting out, "Mum, mum the house is on fire!" Mum rushed back with me and, of course, the house was not on fire, but Tommy was sitting on the bottom of the stairs with his hand up to his left eye and there was a pool of blood on the floor.

Apparently, after catching the lighted match I had attacked him with the knife, stabbing him twice, just above the eyebrow. Thank God it wasn't a fraction below the eyebrow! I really do have no recollection of the actual stabbing, only the panic at seeing the flaming matches arcing across the living room. I do regret that Tommy has carried those scars all his life. Tommy was always a joker, because we had a reunion in Lyle Park in April 2002, about forty old West Silvertown residents turned up and on meeting me again, for the first time in over forty years, Tommy pointed to the scar and said to me, "It's still bleeding!" Tommy had a brother, five years older than us, called Teddy and the three of us had some great times at 11 Westwood Road. We used to have water pistol and red-hot poker fights up and down the stairs. We used saucepan lids as shields and a colander as a helmet. It was always Tommy and I against Teddy. Teddy always had the water pistol and we had the red-hot pokers. I used to put a sheet of newspaper across the open fire-grate to make the wind whistle though the fire and get the pokers even hotter. It's a wonder none of us were seriously injured!

It was a great time with the Batterbee's living upstairs. Tommy's Mum, Bridgette, and his Dad, Ted, used to entertain the drinkers in the Jubilee Pub. Bridgette was an excellent pianist and Ted could both sing and play the drums. Frequently, they would win the Pub raffle and bring the prize home. Generally it was something useful, like a small sack of coal, but one time it was a big white rabbit. I'm not sure if the Pub meant it to be a pet, but the Batterbee's had other ideas. They decided it would make a good stew, or pie, and said that they would kill it with a 'rabbit punch'. First it was young Teddy who held the rabbit suspended by the ears and his Dad got his hand into the classic 'karate chop' shape. Then, while the rabbit was still suspended, after two slow trial runs that stopped just short of the target, he quickly brought the side of his hand in a fast chopping motion across the rabbit's neck.

All hell broke loose! At the point of impact the rabbit wriggled like mad, and its hind legs were going like the clappers. Ted Batterbee let out a loud yell, as clearly he had hurt his hand on the rabbit's neck. They swapped roles and then young Teddy had a go, but with the same result. Both looked puzzled, rubbing the edge of their bruised hands. Then one of them then had the idea of suspending the rabbit and whacking it across the neck with the iron fire poker. The rabbit was still putting up a fight until the poker connected with its neck. It didn't kill it outright, but it stopped all its kicking, shook like mad and its eyes became bulbous. I think at that point I must have left the room. I certainly wasn't there for the kill and later declined a taste of the deceased. As an afterthought, it was a very big rabbit and I think it would have taken them all out in a straight fight!

The Batterbee's were a quite skilled at cooking the local wildlife and they would have made great survivalists. Pigeon pies were one of their favourite dishes. They would place a metal dustbin lid on the ground in the downstairs back yard, supported at an angle by a single thin stick of wood, about a foot in length. The stick would have a length of string attached to it that led up to their upstairs window and some bait was placed under the dustbin lid. Once the pigeon walked under the dustbin lid and started to eat the bait, the string attached to the stick was pulled away and the dustbin lid fell over the unfortunate pigeon. It was then retrieved from under the dustbin lid and killed by having its neck twisted. Then it was de-feathered, washed and placed on a tray in the oven and baked. I never actually ate any of the kills, and as nice as the braised pigeons and pigeon pies looked I could never actually bring myself to taste one. The Batterbee's were re-housed in the mid fifties at number 29 Westwood Road.

Life was very simple in 1950's West Silvertown. Us kids did not need to be amused by television and computer games. I used to play for hours on end with lead model Soldiers or Cowboy and Indian toys, a couple of bundles of wood from which I made a fort, and the elastic bands that had joined the bundles of wood together were used as a sort of slingshot to shoot the Indians. Frequently the heads used to come off the lead soldiers bodies, but as both the heads and bodies were hollow repairs were simple by just inserting a matchstick into the head, then pushing it into the body. We were all 'glued' to the wireless at this period, as television sets were rare in Silvertown. Especially for programmes like Life with the Lyons, Take it from Here, PC Forty-nine, Educating Archie, Ray's a Laugh, Two-way Family Favourites, Dick Barton Special Agent, The Billy Cotton Band Show and the unforgettable 1953 radio series of Journey into Space. This particular programme seemed to captivate the whole of the UK. I'll never forget the adventures of Jet, Doc, Mitch and Lemmy – After the 'James Edward Whittaker' episode I had nightmares for weeks!

One of the games all us kids seemed to prematurely get involved in was playing 'Mums and Dads'. This became one of my favourite early 1950's games. I must have been about seven or eight when I was introduced to this early sexually orientated charade. The game certainly doesn't appear to exist with young children in this 21st Century, but there and again, there is not the acute house over crowding these days with two or three kids sleeping in the same bedroom as their parents. This was mainly, I believe, caused by the trend of having larger families in those days and also the fact that many of our terraced houses had two families living in the same house due to one family having their house destroyed by German air attacks and subsequently being taken in by another family. In such close proximity, sleeping in the same bedroom as their parents, the kids probably both heard and saw what mums and dads got up to and decided to incorporate it into their games. Sometimes we added a bit of variety to the game by playing Tarzan and Nyoka. This was after seeing them both in the Saturday morning kids film shows at the Canning Town Imperial cinema. Tarzan and Nyoka game was very similar to Mums and Dads except it was played in both the gardens and in the Anderson shelters of the bombed houses and on the various debris. I do recall being mildly traumatised one day by a slightly older girl who asked me if I wanted to play mums and dads and then changed it to Tarzan and Nyoka – but she wanted to be Tarzan! I was very confused in the female role of Nyoka, especially when she insisted that we used one of the upturned galvanised metal water tanks that had been blasted into the gardens of the bombed house and she forced me to sit inside. There was just about enough room for me squatting down with my head bent over by the top of the tank. She then wandered off and collected handfuls of the overgrown grass in the deserted garden. I started to get a bit worried that she was going to force me to eat it. When she returned with an armful of grass she then bent down, looked in at me and said, 'Right Nyoka, you've been a very naughty girl and here's your punishment.' She then proceeded to poke all the grass up the top of my thighs, under my short-legged trousers until it was all stuffed under my pants.

I have no idea whatsoever of the pleasure she derived from this strange act, but when my pants were full to bursting and there was no room left to fill, laying there like a stuffed scarecrow; with the grass was spilling out of me, she just got up and walked away. This strange act was never repeated again and whenever I saw this older girl at any future date we both seemed to avert our eyes at the same time. I do hope that she sorted herself out and over the years became more of a Nyoka than Tarzan. Anyway, S-----, if you are reading this, to put your mind at rest, your secret is still safe with me – maybe!

Then there was Lyle Park, and what great times we all had there! It seemed like a meeting place for all the kids in West Silvertown. For many years in the early 1950's I was rarely out of the 'Park House' at number one Bradfield Road. The Boxall and Fisher families lived there and Mr Fisher and Donald Fisher were responsible for the upkeep of Lyle Park. I used to play with Jamie Boxall, usually a game of cowboy's where one of us hid somewhere in the park, usually around the Bandstand at the top, and the other one had to find him without being shot. One Saturday in the early 1950's, after coming back from Saturday morning pictures at the Imperial Cinema at Canning Town, I put a towel around my neck as a cloak, to mimic Captain Marvel who we had just seen in the weekly serial. I then sat on the outside of the window ledge on the first floor of the park house with my arms outstretched, mimicking Captain Marvel, when one of the other kids in the room threw a pillow at me that hit me right in the back catapulting me right out of the window. For a moment I really was Captain Marvel! I never knew that the ground could come up so quickly. I must have been unconscious for a few moments, because the next thing I saw was Mrs Boxall hurrying towards me looking very worried indeed. It would have taken her a few minutes, even at a rushed pace, from the time she was alerted until she had walked through the long park house garden and around the pavilion changing rooms to the back of the house. I felt no pain and I suppose I was quite lucky to have survived the fall.

Mrs Boxall was looking very concerned at my left arm, which had a huge bulge sticking out just above the wrist. It was of course broken. Still no pain, but on seeing the damage I started to cry. I recall Mum rushing me up to Poplar Hospital. Well, as fast as a trolley bus could rush in those days. I was immediately taken from casualty to the operating theatre and will never forget the panic I experienced when a mask was placed over my face to administer the anaesthetic. I remember the buzzing, nausea and numbness of my head, as I appeared to be falling down a hole. I am sure that I wasn't quite unconscious, because I still vividly recall the strange dream I had in the brief period I was 'out' – it was as if I was looking down on my body and seeing one person holding my arm and the other pulling on my wrist. I felt quite sick afterwards. Mum just loved to visit Poplar Hospital and was very well known there. Mum always spent ages at the Hospital snack shop, which was situated in the main hall area and was always involved in long conversations with Mrs Myers, the lady who ran the snack shop. She knew all the names of the Doctors, Sisters and Staff Nurses and delighted in just greeting them. Hospital visits were always a great day out for Mum and she really did seem to enjoy them. I think it was the closest she ever got to Butlins Holiday Camp!

Most of us kids had a whale of a time playing in the bombed houses in the early 1950's. I was lucky enough to have two directly opposite, remnants from the 7th September 1940 first night of German air raids when mum was blown down the passageway and into the scullery. I thoroughly enjoyed climbing up what was left of the stairs, jumping across the joists on the first floor, as there were no floor boards, and climbing into the beamed area where there used to be a tiled roof. This was a common practice for all the kids and our parents seemed oblivious to the dangers. We'd be playing a game of 'he', leaping across joists on the first floor of the house where the floor boards, or ceilings used to be, and Mum would be calling up from the street below 'Stanley, tea is in 10 minutes, don't be late.' These days the areas would be fenced off as a real Health and Safety nightmare zone!

The very best bombed houses, which were an absolute magnet for all the children, were situated in Knights Road. We all enjoyed having stone throwing and catapult fights with some kids standing within the exposed roof cavities of the bombed houses and others shooting stones upwards from the Anderson shelters that had been dug into the back gardens. Remarkably, serious accidents were rare but this was most certainly due more to luck rather than our judgement. We also used to make very effective spears from the thin lathes of wood that we used to pull out from under the plaster covering the walls of the bombed houses. Once the lathes were split into three or four lengths, one end would be sharpened to a fine point and the other end would have a paper flight fitted, similar to the flights used in darts. In order to balance the spear we would rip out the rubber covered electric wire from above the ceilings, tear off the rubber sleeve and wrap the wire around just above the pointed end. They were deadly! I remember that in one 'battle' on the large debri between the end of Knights Road and Bradfield Road I threw my spear high in the air towards Roy Harris. Generally, we would see the spears coming and move out of the flight path, but on this occasion Roy must have lost concentration. I was horrified when it embedded itself in his forehead, just above the eyeline. I ran away, but fortunately he was not seriously injured.

All this skylarking about did unfortunately result in a serious injury for one of the boys. It was Terry Farmer from Cranbrook Road. I knew the family quite well because Terry's dad, Steve Farmer ran a loan club and I used to take both mum and nan's weekly payment round to their house. The accident happened on the roof of the Chapel at the end of Westwood Road, on the opposite corner to the Jubilee Public House. The Chapel was abandoned and semi-dilapidated and in later years was turned into yet another Silvertown Café. Wrought iron railings bordered the Café, with a sharp spike at the top of each railing. We all used to play games around the Chapel, scrambling over the roof playing 'He' and throwing stones at each other. On this occasion Terry lost his footing on the sloped slate roof and fell over the side landing right on top of one of the spikes. The spike penetrated deep into his backside. He was completely impaled and regulars at the Jubilee Pub rushed across to his assistance, lifting him off. Terry was extremely lucky to have survived the fall, let alone the impalement on the spike.

Stan Dyson

Another area that we congregated was right at the very end of Bradfield Road that we called 'the bank' and also 'the river steps.' It was past the Shell-Mex Petroleum and Vigzol Oil factories and was a narrow passageway that led you to two flights of wooden steps that ended directly into the Thames or onto the very deep river bank mud if the tide was out. When the tide was in we used to really chance our arm by swinging out over the Thames on a piece of thick rope that was generally used to berth both ships and barges. One slip in the wrong direction and you would be dunked in the Thames and immediately swept by the strong currents under the barges, or boats, moored to the jetty to a swift and certain death. In the right direction, providing your mates caught you, the worse you'd get is soaking wet. So there was a lot of kudos in having the 'bottle' to take the running jump off the steps and launch yourself at the rope, hoping your luck was in. Not everyone took advantage of this, but I always did because I enjoyed that 'tingling' sensation you got just as you took off from the steps trusting in both your luck and judgement. Floating peanuts always seemed to congregate in the gap at the river steps when the tide was in and we used to scoop them out of the water, split the damp shells, and eat them with relish. Although they had been floating in the polluted Thames for probably some time we never became ill and neither did we for one moment wonder where they all came from in the first place.

Sometimes we spent time excavating the earth wall either side of the River Steps. It may have been some sort of landfill area many years earlier, because we used to dig small bones, bits of china and small bottles out of the earth walls. We just tossed the occasional small green bottles we dug out into the Thames. They would probably be worth some money today. The entrance to the River Steps has now been sealed off, but prior to this I noticed during my last visit in 1991 that both sides of the earth walls had been covered and reinforced with concrete. Perhaps we dug too deep in some areas.

2

Comic Catastrophe

Swapping comics with other kids was another popular pastime. This was more out of necessity than choice, because nobody living in our area was particularly affluent and by swapping comics with your friends you saved valuable family cash and were able to read more comics than you could ever have afforded to purchase. Initially, it was just the Dandy, Beano, Knockout, both Radio and Film Fun and then came The Eagle, Topper, and the Beezer. In 1955/56 I became hooked on the more sinister comics like The Phantom and also 'Black Magic', the comic that was deemed to be so sinister that it was actually banned. I was also into Captain Video, Captain Marvel and Superman comics and after 1957 the Hotspur and Wizard. It was around the time of 1954, when I first introduced my young sister, Kathleen, into comic swapping. Given that we were all relatively poor in our area, swopping comics was a great way to benefit from reading most of the comics without actually incurring the cost. We went to one of the houses in Barnwood Road and Kathy did a particularly good swap, so on our way back home, at the corner of Barnwood Road, I gave her a hug and a big kiss on the cheek and said "Well Done!" As she stood there, with her red scarf wrapped around her neck, I can still see her huge smile and face glowing with pride.

Comics did cause quite a tragic accident in our house in the early 1950's. Neither Kathy nor me liked the Dandy as much as the Beano. In those days there was no such thing as central heating. At that particular time in our house we only kept a fire in the middle living room. A tiled fireplace surrounded the fire with raised concrete tile-covered plinths at either end that kids could comfortably sit on. The fires were huge, but as the wind used to whistle through the gaps in the doors, so if you sat on the door sided plinth then you roasted at the front and got a cold draught up your back. However, if you sat on the other side it was pure bliss. We shared the middle bedroom upstairs, and we could hear when the newspaper and comics were delivered, so there was always a double rush on Dandy & Beano day. Neither of us wanted to either read the Dandy first or sit on the door side of the tiled fireplace plinth.

We did not have an electric iron; neither did most of the West Silvertown residents. Mum always had two flat irons on the go when she was ironing using one of them to iron while the other one was 'hotting-up' on the gas ring. Mum used to put a solid flat iron on the gas stove in the scullery and pick it up by the handle holding a folded damp flannel as protection from the extremely hot handle. She always used to test it first on an old piece of linen, because with no temperature control quite often it was so hot that it would scorch the fabric. If the iron did scorch the fabric then Mum would place it onto the tiled plinth to cool down. When the iron cooled too much she would take it down the passage to the scullery, remove the searing hot iron and place the warm one back onto the gas stove. This particular morning Mum had started her ironing early and had been storing the 'too hot' iron on the tiled plinth for quite some time. Unfortunately, the comics arrived through the letterbox at the same time as Mum retrieved the 'mad hot' flat iron from the tiled plinth that surrounded the open fire in the hearth.

As we heard the comics drop through the letterbox we both leapt out of our beds and made a rush for the bedroom door. It was neck and neck down the stairs, but I just managed to get to the comics first. I got the Beano, threw the Dandy up the stairs to ensure I won the second part of the race for the coveted right hand side plinth. I sat down in my pyjamas and laughed. Kathy came in clutching the Dandy, with the sulkiest look you could imagine. She stomped over to the door side plinth, pulled up her nightdress to waist height and promptly sat down on the tiled plinth. It was flesh straight onto the unbelievably hot tiled plinth. I can still hear her scream and see her jumping high into the air and running around the room clutching her bottom screaming. Initially I laughed, because I had no idea what had happened and the damage that had been done. It soon became apparent that it was serious, which immediately curtailed my laughter. Kathy was admitted into Poplar Hospital and was kept in for some days.

That was the very last time that I ever got involved in the 'comic race' and I am sorry that I won the race that ended in Kathy being so severely burned. If I had lost the race at least I would have had the added protection of my thick cotton pyjamas between the plinth and me, instead of just bare flesh.

3

The shops and local industry

Money seemed to go a long way in the early 1950's. Gladys and Dorothy Hobbs ran the Grocery and Provisions shop on the corner of Eastwood Road. I used to enjoy buying a penny glass of Tizer and Gladys always threw in some free coconut strands that had fallen off the pile of icing covered cheesecakes. On the opposite corner of Eastwood Road, right next to the Doctors Surgery, there was the Electric and Radio shop run by Alec and Joyce King. Whenever something went wrong with our large black Bakelite 'wireless' it was always rushed round to Alec King's for repair. Unfortunately, the valves in the wireless did not seem last very long and I was a regular visitor to the King's for replacement valves. You could still spend a farthing on sweets in Alf and Mick Knightly's confectionery and tobacco shop buying blackjacks and fruit salad sweets. Ted Manning owned the Fish Shop and always produced unforgettable battered and fried skate; although I really enjoyed the meaty top layer of the skate I could never really enjoy the thinner slimy underside of the skate. Poor Ted was crippled by some sort of spinal disability therefore had mobility problems, but that did not stop him producing some of the best fish and chips I've ever tasted. Ted cooked the lot, Cod, Haddock, Skate, Plaice, Rock Eel and Roe. He had a very loud, deep, gruff voice and frightened me a bit as a kid, but later, as I grew into my teen years I realised what a great sense of humour he had and what a joker he was. Next door to Ted's fish shop there was the Barber Shop run by Charlie Allen and Jack Monroe. As us lads sat there, waiting for our turn, we always talked about how West Ham United Football Club were doing. The standard joke was 'Why did WHUFC Manager give all his players a lighter each?' Answer, 'Because they keep loosing their matches!' At the end of each of the men's haircuts Charlie Allen would always ask 'Would you like a singe Sir?' The 'singe' always fascinated me, because as Charlie lit the wax taper and ran it across the top of the customer's head their hair actually caught fire! After this, Charlie would lean forward and softly whisper in their ear, 'Anything for the weekend Sir?' I could understand why Charlie never asked us kids about a singe, but I was puzzled why he didn't ask if we wanted anything for the weekend. A nice packet of spangles or Rountree's fruit gums would have gone down a treat! Right next to the Barbers shop was Evans Dairy and next to that on the corner of Barnwood Road was Legg's the Butchers Shop.

On the opposite corner of Barnwood Road was Ray Giffiths Grocery and Provisions shop, but this closed around the mid 1950's and became a ladies hairdressing shop called 'Iris Hairdressers' owned I believe by Iris Bullard. Next to that was Jean Docherty's Newsagent and Tobacconist shop. Jean was a dour Scot and could be quite sharp at times, although in my years working for her as a paper-boy I realise she was, despite being a Scot, quite generous and had a heart of gold. Then there was the Post Office that in the 1950's to the very best of my memory was run by Doug Scott. A great guy, who was always cheerful and ready for a joke and he was assisted on the haberdashery and stationary side of the shop by Mrs Bull from Bradfield Road. Then there was Mantons Sweet Shop, which then became Walkers and finally the Richardson's ran it. After the Café, which was run by Agnes and George Beckford, there was Kate Pattison's Green Grocery shop, then finally, on the corner of Eastwood Road was the shop that supplied most of the grocery and provisions to the whole area. Although, in the early 1950's, Gladys and Dorothy Hobbs owned this shop, but by the mid 1950's it was taken over by John and Amy Pattison until such time as it was demolished in the early 1960's.

Stan Dyson

There were five café's in West Silvertown. The first was on the corner of Cranbrook Road, followed by one on the next corner in Barnwood Road, then another midway between the parade of shops from Barnwood Road to Eastwood Road, right next to Mantons. We had one at the top of Westwood Road, right next door to the Jubilee Public House and on the other corner of Westwood Road opposite the Jubilee there was another one situated by the bus stop. This last one was formerly the local Chapel. Ernie and Isobel Gallerfing owned the café at the Westwood Road. Bridgette Batterbee, who you will recall lived upstairs in our house, worked in the Gallerfing's' Café therefore I was a frequent visitor to the Café. They also had a daughter called Wendy, who at times played with my sister Kathy. Because of the Café' the top end of Westwood Road was always occupied by parked lorries as their drivers indulged themselves in breakfast and lunch.

Us kids were always 'curious' as to the content of the parked lorries and frequently 'investigated' while the drivers were having their meals. There was a family living in Evelyn Road who had three boys, all of who were older than me. They were quite 'adventurous' and were looked upon as very tough. I believe they were either Daltons or Pearsons and they had opened, and were emptying, the content of some of the hessian sacks of brown granulated sugar from the back of one of the parked Tate & Lyle lorries by cutting holes in the sack and collecting the spillage into boxes. I livened up the day by going into the Café and asking Bridgette Batterbee who was driving the sugar lorry. Bridgette made a loud verbal enquiry and when the driver and his mate identified themselves I advised them of the situation. They leapt up and ran into the street chasing the three culprits. One boy ran straight for home and the other two ran across the debri opposite and into the two dilapidated bombed houses.

The two men chased the boys into the bombed houses. As the houses were just shells the chase was open for all to see. There was no 'I know my rights' and 'you can't lay a hand on me' kind of talkback in those days. Summary justice was the order of the day and it was dished out on the spot! The chase across what was left of the roof of the two-bombed houses had by now attracted quite a crowd, who had followed the pursuit across the debri in Westwood Road to Hanameel Street. One of the boys tried to get out of the upstairs window of the house onto the roof of the adjacent chapel. He was 'collared' halfway through the window by one of the men and dragged back into the house. After a few thuds and slaps, grunts, groans and 'ouches' he was then literally dragged out of the bombed house by the angry driver. At this stage I was so frightened of the consequence of my 'grassing-up' the brothers that I ran back indoors and hid under the table. Bridgette came into the house moments later and told my Mum that the men would like to personally thank me.

Although Mum was quite pleased that I had performed this public service I clung onto the table leg for dear life. If the brothers ever found out that it was me that fingered them I was doomed. I was worried for days after that and I hope they are not reading this account of the incident today! On my next visit to the Café Isobel Gallerfing said "I've got something for you Stanley." She produced a beautiful looking silver Wild West toy revolver. I stared at it mesmerised, until she pulled the trigger! There was a small flash and a loud bang – it had caps! I had a morbid fear of thunderstorms at that period of my life and hated any kind of bangs, so although the gun was given to my Mum it was quite some time before I had the courage to play with it. I have a suspicion that this fear of loud bangs in my young years was something to do with the terror mum endured during the time she was pregnant with me and hiding night after night under the Silvertown arches while we were under the intense German aerial bombardment.

We also had various types of street traders in the 1950's. A fairly regular street trader of the time was the knife sharpener. All us kids looked forward to his visit. He had a bicycle contraption that had a large box fitted around the handlebar area with a huge round sharpening stone, looking something like a millstone, fixed upright in the middle. We would all rush out and hand him our blunt carving knives and peddling away he would make the sharpening stone spin faster and faster, at which point upon applying the knife to the spinning stone there would be a shower of sparks – this is just what we were all waiting for! Then there was the large bearded Sikh who always wore a turban and sold men's neckties and ladies silk scarves from a huge suitcase crammed full of his wares. It was always a bit of a job getting rid of him, because his mastery of English was not that good. By far our favourite was Leo, the ragman. His real name was Levi Lee, but we always called him Leo. A tall slim man of Gypsy descent. He had a well-tanned weather worn face with a pencil moustache, prominent cheekbones and deep-set dark eyes. From memory he always wore a double-breasted pinstriped jacket with a red Romany type necktie. I did hear a story that in the First World War Leo helped the British Forces by breaking in wild horses for the cavalry. Sometimes he would walk the streets of Canning Town and Silvertown with his horse and cart shouting out, 'Old rags for china, old rags for china.' We would then rush out with all our discarded bits and pieces of clothing and Leo would give us a china cup, saucer or plate in exchange. Other times he would come around with Goldfish in exchange for the rags. During the summer months Leo would alternate the rag days with a rickety child's roundabout, again pulled by his pony. I believe it was a penny a ride. We would hand Leo our penny and clutching on for dear life we would sit in the small contraption while Leo manually turned the handle and the roundabout spun around, sometimes at a worrying angle!

The summers seemed very long in the early 1950's and very hot, sometimes the tar on the pavement would actually bubble up. This all added to the general 'stink' of Silvertown. With the heavy industry, all geared to production, Silvertown had a smell all of its own. Right next to Tate & Lyle, who were handling sugar and producing sweet smelling syrup and molasses, was John Knights soap factory. Soap, as we all know is produced from the carcasses of rendered down dead animal bones and John Knights had animal carcasses stacked up like mountains. I am sure that if half the country that was using the well advertised and popular 'Knights Castille' soap had ever walked down smelly Knights Road and seen the mountains of animal carcasses that produced the soap they would have immediately discontinued its use.

You can imagine that in the hot summer time the smell was awful, although, funny enough, you did get used to it. The upside of this, for us kids, was that given all the animal skeletons stacked sky high, there were bluebottles almost the size of small birds on the walls the whole length of Knights Road. A favourite summer pursuit was 'fly swatting'. It was easy to get a rolled up newspaper and just squash them up against the wall. There was no skill in that. The skilful exercise was to take some of the long thick rubber bands that joined the bundles of fire wood, cut and knot them together and you had a great slingshot that you could pull back, like a bow and arrow, close one eye, aim and fire. As the loose end of the rubber band struck its target the bluebottle would explode against the wall like a red, yellow, blue mixture paintball. The only problem is, as you may have guessed, after the first strike your index finger and thumb would be holding the very part of the rubber band that had just squashed the bluebottle to infinity. By the time I had shot my way from the start of Knights Road to the end of Knights road my thumb and index finger would be blood red with dark flecks of bluebottle legs and wings attached. At the end of the shoot-up I always had a quick sniff of my fingers and they stunk. A quite unbelievable smell! Yet it never ever bothered us. I would just spit on my fingers and wipe them on small turf's of grass in the pavement or kerb. Lyle Park was just across the bombsite debri at the end of Knights Road, so occasionally I would go into the park and just run my fingers under the cold drinking water fountain. Then home for a quick sandwich – there was no instant hot water and disinfectant in our house!

West Silvertown became almost silent during the weekends. With all the heavy industry weekdays were quite frantic with all the workers having lunch in the café's and also buying items in the parade of shops. The Victoria Dock and factories Tate & Lyle, Pinchin Johnsons, British Oil and Cake Mills, John Knights, Venesta's and Ranks & Spillers Flour Mills were tightly packed in an area under one mile. Although the area was never congested with cars, as it is nowadays, factory workers were everywhere. In all probability they all came to work on the 669 trolley buses and from the mid 1950's the new diesel 69 Routemaster buses. Even though most of the large industry had a works canteen, the café's along the North Woolwich Road were always packed out. Some of the larger factories like Lyles even had their own Sports & Recreation Club, so after dining in the canteen you could work it off afterwards with a game of table tennis, darts or snooker or there was always Lyle Park for a kick around with a football before returning to work.

4

School life and Beanos

School life progressed and I moved up to the second class with Miss Sigenham, a tall nice looking ash blonde teacher. Although it was not as laid back and fun-filled as Miss Peacock's class my limited recollections were that it was quite enjoyable. At last we had really started real reading, writing and arithmetic. We were also allowed now to go into the 'Model Room' and use the wet clay to mould into model animals, vases and plates. Miss Empson, later to become, Mrs Pearson was the headmistress. A very well spoken and dignified lady around mid forties, who looked quite stern, was fairly strict but at the same time very fair. Mum got on very well with Miss Empson and so did I.

One thing I did enjoy at this period was lighting fires as I was, although fearful, at the same time really fascinated by fire. I used to hang about outside the Jubilee pub and ask some of the men who were drinking their pints of bitter, or mild and bitter, (there were no lagers then) if they could set light to a piece of paper that I had placed into the kerb. This graduated to pinching one of Mums boxes of matches and setting fire to rubbish that I had placed on the various bombsites that still surrounded war damaged Silvertown. I would then rush around to the fire station, at the top of Mill Road, ring the bell and tell them that there was a fire. That got me a very exciting ride at the front of the fire engine to point out where the fire was blazing away. Needless to say that after a few rides they soon twigged my ruse and after having a very stern warning from the station fire officer I ceased this enjoyable past time.

The Jubilee was quite a hang-about area for us kids, especially at 'Beano' time, when all the regulars would go on a days outing to either Southend-on-Sea or Margate. This was usually quite early in the morning, I would guess around 7.30am to 8.30am. I once went to see them off in my pyjamas with my long mackintosh over the top. The reason us kids went to see them off was that just before the coach left the Pub we would all shout "Throw out your mouldies." The windows of the coach were opened and the adults would all start to throw out handfuls of pennies and halfpennies. Once I actually got a threepenny piece. The Beano's were rarely mixed affairs. They always seemed to be either entirely male or female days out.

Being so close to the docks we always had a variety of different nationalities of seamen and foreign visitors. One of my early hobbies was collecting foreign matchboxes and coins. I used to wait outside the Victoria Dock entrance gate in Mill Road and as foreigners came out I would shout, "Got any foreign match boxes or coins please mister?" Quite often we would squeeze through a hole in the Victoria Dock fence and walk to the side of the jetties by the ships, seeing if we could match the ship to our collection of steamship post cards, or if we saw any of the seamen looking over the side of the ships we would just stand there shouting up, 'Any foreign match boxes or money mister?' Invariably, the patrolling dock policeman soon spotted us and chased us out.

Once while about six of us boys were standing on the corner of Westwood Road, just outside the Jubilee pub when a tall American man, about fifty years of age, came up and started talking to us. He was telling us about a young boy 'genius' back in the USA. I clearly remember that he said they called him 'young Einstein'. I had never heard the name 'Einstein' before and, as the two syllables rhymed, it stayed with me over the years. He went on to say that he could accurately predict the precise age of each of us by feeling the muscles in our legs. He said that as boys got older the muscles became harder. He said that we must not cheat by tensing our leg muscles to make

Men's Jubilee Pub Beano 1950's

ourselves appear older than we were. We were all keen to have a go and luckily (or unluckily, as the case may be) he chose me first. I felt quite proud of this and of course I tensed like mad. I was nine years of age at the time. He knelt down to my height and felt around my calves, then slowly progressed right up above the back of my knee to my thighs. He seemed to be really concentrating on the job in hand.

"How old am I then mister?" I said, tensing my thighs even harder. I recall him saying "Hmm, difficult, this one." Going up higher, just under my short trousers. "Hurry up, I'm next." Said one of the others, anxiously. I tensed even harder, until my legs were almost shaking. I recall thinking that I could not keep this up much longer, but quite pleased that he could not easily guess my age. "How old then mister?" I repeated. He didn't answer, but his hands were now well underneath my short trousers. 'Nearly touching my winkie now', I thought. He was looking at me eye to eye as he conducted his examination of the very top of my thighs and he must have seen the apprehension in my eyes. He suddenly stopped and stood up. At last I could relax my calves and thighs. "How old am I then?" I persisted. He stood up and I recall him saying quite clearly "I would say you are about fourteen years of age."

Ladies Jubilee Pub Beano 1950's

"No!" I shouted, "I'm nine." I was elated and I felt so special that he had got my age wrong by thinking that I was much older than my years. He then turned to one of the others and knelt down to feel his thighs. At that point two of the Jubilee regulars came up and asked him what he was doing. Although he endeavoured to explain it to them, he did not achieve the same success as he had with us boys. I clearly recall one of them said; quite rudely I thought at the time, "I think you better fuck off mate!" Needless to say, he disappeared fairly quickly. Funny the way some seemingly insignificant incidents stay with you so clearly through your life. I realise now, of course, that I had just given some American paedophile the time of his life!

At nine years of age I was in Mr Davis's class. I recall it with horror! He called us all "mister", generally at about 120 decibels, shouting, "What do you think you're doing mister?" It was said that he was an ex sergeant major from the army and he certainly looked and acted like one. Being in his class was pure hell, especially if he had it in for you. I hated it! If you did not quite understand something he seemed to have thought that you would if he shouted loud enough just six inches from your face. I remember that he made poor George Beautyman's life hell. I recall George's Mum, Daisy, Storming in the classroom and having a good scream at him, finally turning her back on him, bending over at the same time she pulled up her skirt shouting "You can axe my arse!" He certainly made me very nervous, but never mind, because his come-uppance from me would come many years later.

We had one family in Westwood Road where the father had a debilitating illness. I believe that it was motor-neurone disease, or multiple sclerosis. He had five daughters, Ruby, Sylvia, Vera, Brenda and the youngest Gloria. Gloria was very friendly with my sister. In fact, Gloria was the very first girl I ever kissed. I was about seven or eight years of age and half dozen of us were in Lyle Park, sitting in the park hut next to the Bandstand overlooking the Thames. We were all playing 'dares and forfeits' and my one was to kiss Gloria. I can still see her face screwing up, almost flinching, as she presented me with her cheek. Gloria was best of friends with my sister Kathy and was frequently in our house and in later years accompanied us on our days out to Southend-on-Sea. I was very fond of Gloria's Dad, 'Uncle Charlie', as I called him, and can well recall the magic tricks he used to show me as he sat on the wall outside his house. I never tired of the disappearing marble trick. Uncle Charlie used to spend a lot of time chatting with the Park Keepers in Lyle Park, Mr Ricketts and Mr Creagan. He used to travel the quarter mile journey from Westwood Road to Lyle Park by a motorised wheel chair. Despite his increasing debilitating illness, Charlie was always so cheerful. Sadly, in the 1960's Charlie took his own life by swallowing a particularly painful poison. It was done in the family home and witnessed by his wife and daughters. It was a tragedy that stayed with us all for a long time and Charlie was sadly missed, not just by the residents of Westwood Road, but also by all in the West Silvertown Hamlet that had known him. I agonised for a long time how he had found the courage to the swallow that corrosive liquid.

5

Family life and Rathbone Street shopping

My Nan and Grandad, Alice and Jim Guinee, lived next door but one, at number 15 Westwood Road. In Earlier years, when Mum was a child, they had lived at number 17, where the Taylor family currently lived. Mum had three brothers, James, Daniel and Cornelius. Jimmy was married and lived in Chesterton Terrace, Plaistow, and in the early 1950's Danny and Con stilled lived at home. Nan was a regular Churchgoer and very involved in the local St Barnabus Church affairs and she was also involved with the West Ham Central Mission. She had been in domestic service when she met Granddad. He had come to England from Cork and around 1910 they lived at 3 North Woolwich Road, one of the houses directly opposite The Ram Public House. Granddad had fought in France in the First World War, serving as a Sergeant in the Royal Irish Rifles and he still looked the part with his military type moustache. Originally he worked as a blender in Pinchin Johnsons paint factory and then for many years as Yard Gang Foreman at Tate and Lyle, Plaistow Wharf Refinery. After he retired in the early 1950's he was presented with a long service award and then became the 'character' pot-man in the Jubilee Public House for many years.

My Uncle Dan really was a problem to the family. He was quite well built, with dark brown hair, craggy weather worn face and a couldn't care-a-less attitude towards both life and the local community. He was a very heavy beer drinker and was frequently drunk and standing just outside the Jubilee Tavern looking for an argument or fight with whoever walked past him. The excuse given for his behaviour was that in his younger days, as a motorcycle passenger, he was involved in a crash that resulted in an injury to his head. Later, whilst working on a building site, scaffolding collapsed and fell on him, again injuring his head. Then, at Canning Town, in his rush to cross the road from Canning Town Railway Station to the Liverpool Arms Pub he misjudged his footing, slipped forward, and a bus caught him a glancing blow to his head. He then became a very heavy drinker and, because of his anti social behaviour, was barred from most of the pubs in the area. Outside of drink he was great. I really liked him, but in his drunken state he was one of your worst nightmares. He would pick a fight with anyone who gave him a wrong look in the pub. When Jubilee pub landlord, Eric Bowden, ejected him he would then stand at the bus-top outside the café, at the end of Westwood Road, and try and pick a fight with bus conductors, or any unfortunate locals that got of at that particular stop. Danny was usually unemployed, and to feed his drinking habit he would break open Nan's gas and electric meters, steal the contents, then he would disappear for days until the heat had gone down.

Danny did come quite a cropper once though. The Richardsons, who were not locals, had purchased Mantons Sweet Shop that was being run by Mrs Walker who lived at 5 Westwood Road. Coincidentally, me and their son Allen, attended South West Ham Technical School, and Allen used to relate stories about his dad's activities in the Second World War. Apparently he was a paratrooper or commando in Special Forces. All the locals would give Danny a wide berth when he was in his drunken state, but of course Mr Richardson has absolutely no idea about Danny or his reputation. There he was, standing by the door of his sweet shop, when Danny came up to pick a fight. Apparently, after goading Mr Richardson Danny drew back his fist for what he thought would be an easy conquest, at which point Mr Richardson's right hand connected with Danny's jaw. Danny was instantly knocked out and lying prone on the pavement. Although Danny could not recall what

The busy Rathbone Street Market 1950"s

had happened after he regained consciousness he did return to Mr Richardson the following day to apologise.

Mum and me had great shopping trips to Rathbone Street market in Canning Town. These represent some of my earliest memories and it's funny that the most insignificant of events stick in your mind. I remember mum pushing me back from Rathbone Street in a pushchair and coming down the viaduct at the Victoria Dock entrance just opposite Lyles syrup factory. I would have been under two years of age and Peggy Stocks and her daughter Carol, who was born just four days before me, accompanied us. Our mothers were probably in Forest Gate Maternity Hospital at the same time, which may have accounted for the friendship. Always, after reaching the bottom of the Silvertwown Viaduct we would call in at their house at 28 Cranbrook Road for a drink and I remember thinking how dark it seemed to be in their house compared with ours.

Rathbone Street was a vibrant East End market and a fun place to be with mum. We generally started the shopping at Davies's Bacon and Provisions shop end of the market, opposite Cribbs funeral parlour. This was a large combined butchers and grocery store that was owned by a man called William Davies. Mrs Ripp or George, a coloured guy who was always joking and very popular, would always serve mum with her grocery provisions then she would move over to the other side of the shop and buy her cooked meats, like ham or spam, from John Ripp, who managed the shop. We would then move further down the market to Bill Webb's butchers shop, passing on the way Frank Wises' biscuit stall. Frank was constantly verbally plying his platter to all passing shoppers, without a pause for breath – he did a roaring trade in broken biscuits and sold the very best hot-cross buns I have ever tasted. Frank, due to his non-stop sales talk, frequently had a smear of foam in the corner of his mouth, and this fascinated me. We would then move on past Thakes fish stall. I just had to stop here and watch the live eels, coated in slime and slithering all over each other. Mum got a bit impatient here, because I just had to wait for someone to buy the eels. They were weighed then, still wriggling, had their heads cut off with a sharp knife.

Moving further down the market we may, if we were unlucky enough, have to stop at Alexandra's Cobbler shop. Poor old Mr Alec (as we called him) was absolutely surrounded by shoes. It seemed that quite often, after a long search, he would eventually find your shoes, that may have been there for a week or more and say, "Yes, they will be ready for you tomorrow." Other times, after the shoes were described to him he may lift up several similar types, only for mum to impatiently say "No!" Then he would find one and mum would say "Yes that's one of them!" The search would continue across the floor of the shop, amongst the shoes littered everywhere. It may even extend through the door into the living area of the shop, at which point Mr Alec would triumphantly re-appear with the missing shoe, again stating 'They'll be ready for tomorrow.' Alexandra's also sold all types of purses and bags from a stool outside the shop. Little did I know at that time that at the age of fifteen I would be helping out Friday nights on my way home from school every Friday afternoon, packing all the bags away and wheeling the stool to it's parking area further down the road. I also worked some Saturday mornings selling the bags outside the shop, shouting out "Two bob a bag, any colour you like, only two-bob a bag." Then, after leaving Alexandra's we would walk past Mudies Herbal Store. In the winter months I could not pass this point without pestering mum for a hot Sarsaparilla drink. That unforgettable taste was pure magic!

We would pass Hymie Secunda's drapery and outfitters shop and his two market stools. I also worked on his stool during my last year at school in 1961 selling men's jeans and underwear. Mum frequently went into Wicks Haberdashery shop, on the corner of Fox Street, almost opposite Caters. It was a long narrow shop and the floorboards creaked and echoed loudly until you reached the counter at the end. Then you were met by the strangest of ladies, who both fascinated and frightened me. I can still vividly recall her today. Very tall and extremely thin, clearly Jewish, with quite a lot of make-up and very dark hair, cut almost to a skinhead. She also wore thick horn rimmed 'Buddy Holly' type glasses. She certainly appeared well ahead of her time, in what must have been 1952/3. We usually ended up in Mrs Olley's Pie and Mash shop. There was a large talking parrot in a cage suspended from the ceiling towards the end of the shop and it used to shout out "Gis a bit!" The crusty topped meat pie, mash and green parsley liquor served up by Mrs Olley was absolutely superb, especially after you had doused it with pepper and vinegar. If you were unlucky enough to be sitting by the cage end of the shop when the parrot decided to exercise its wings all manner of droppings and feathers would erupt from the cage. At this point we all did our best to cover our meal as the airburst dissipated over the tables, but at the end of the day I suppose it all added to the flavour. The day would be rounded off with a Murkoffs ice cream cornet. Murkoff's was situated in Barking Road, by the bus stop immediately opposite Canning Town Public Hall, and in my opinion undeniably sold the best tasting ice cream in the world!

At the very start of Rathbone Street Market, opposite the Ordnance public house in the Barking Road, there was a huge debri that was absolutely littered with second hand market traders. They did not have stalls like the bona fide market traders, but just scattered their wares either directly onto the ground, or on top of a tarpaulin or a large sheet. They were like a magnet to the foreign seamen who, bartering like mad, flocked around them. The Indian seamen, or Lascars, as we called them, always fascinated me. They bought all manner of odds and ends on that debri that you would never think were remotely saleable, like huge bundles of old clothes tied together with string, old tea chest trunks and clapped out old bicycles. They always seemed to walk back to the Victoria Dock in a long single file up the Canning Town Viaduct, just pushing their bicycles; with the bundles of old clothes held on their heads and to me really did look a strange site, even in mid 1950's East London Docklands.

Christmas Eve in Rathbone Street was pure magic. It was so unbelievably crowded and there was a real buzz, what with all the excitement of the festive season and the stools brightly lit with bulbs and Christmas decorations; and the stall holders shouting out loud to attract more customers. It was around the 1955 period that dad gave me thirty shillings on Christmas Eve and trusted me to take my sister Kathy to Rathbone Street and buy last minute items and Christmas decorations. Thirty shillings was a lot of money in those days and I was absolutely delighted that I had been trusted to shop sensibly and take good care of my sister. We had a great time in Rathbone Street, buying various small Christmas novelties, and had progressed into Barking Road where I spent money on the most expensive item, a stereo viewer with various photos to view as three-dimensional images, costing seven shillings and six pence in Feldmans Chemist shop. We had been gone for hours and, quite worried, dad came looking for us. He found us in Woolworth's, hearing my loud voice calling to the shop assistant "Can you serve the girl please."

Christmas was a great time in our house. It was one of the only times we really got to eat fruit! Mum would order a large box of fruit from Mrs Pattisons green grocery shop. We gorged on tangerines, apples, oranges and bananas. We also had a whole bottle of Ribena black currant drink to dilute with the cold water from the tap. One Christmas Mrs Pattison completely forgot both Mum and Nan's order and they had to go round and knock her up after closing time. Mum said that Mrs Pattison liked a tipple and must have overdone it and just fallen asleep, forgetting our Christmas delivery order. As a real treat we would really look forward to the large chicken that mum would have bought from Bill Webb, the Butcher in Rathbone Street. Chicken was a real luxury in the 1950's and generally, unless you were really rich, only eaten at Christmas. The usual Sunday lunch for the other 51 weeks of the year was roast beef, always served at the table as we listened to the 12-noon radio program Two Way Family Favourites. I

Silvertown Life

Rathbone Streeet Market 1956

never really believed in Father Christmas and always waited for dad to come upstairs and place a pillowcase of goodies at the end of my bed. I would then carefully search the content of the pillowcase in the pitch black of the bedroom; consume the tangerine, an orange and couple of silver covered milk chocolate coins that had been previously hanging on the Christmas tree. I would then try and identify the toys by feeling them in the dark.

Weekday meals in our house were an odd affair in the 1950's. I remember my dinner, taken at lunchtime, was quite often a whole tin of Heinz tomato soup with loads of slices of bread, sometimes accompanied with slices of cheddar cheese. I loved it, but it did get a bit monotonous. By 1955 I was allowed to choose my own lunch time meal, the only meal I got all day, as we only had a bread and jam snack in the evening at 'tea-time', as we called it. For many months the meal of my choice was a Lyons square individual fruit pie covered in evaporated milk. The only meal I feared was my Nan's lamb stew. I hated it! I would have been around five or six years of age and I was usually in my Nan's house at 15 Westwood Road. I guess Nan must have cooked a huge one for the whole family, served onto the plate direct from a large saucepan. There was always a fine layer of congealed fat on the surface, like thin ice across a puddle on a frosty morning. I can still recall mum picking up lumps of the fatty lamb to force into my mouth. The awful smell of the lamb on her fingers still haunts me today – I would very nearly throw up! On the positive side mum did make an out of this world 'cheese in milk' dish, which was literally just thin slices of cheese in a large saucer of milk put straight onto a 'low glimmer' of gas and left to melt and then eaten as a dip with slices of buttered bread. Also, to this day, nobody has ever beaten mum's sausage, mash and fried onion's. A dish to die for!

Sunday's were always a special day for us kids in the 1950's because we all looked forward to, and indulged ourselves, in our traditional English Sunday roast beef dinner. The preparations started quite early in the morning with mum preparing the vegetables. There were the potatoes for roasting in the oven with the beef, and pea's, parsnips, carrots and the one vegetable I really hated was brussel sprouts, but we only ate them at certain times when they were in season. I always enjoyed helping out here by shelling the peas, but I must say that almost as many went into my mouth as into the pot, because it was a sheer joy chewing on those fresh young pea's as you popped them straight out of the pod. Mum also cooked a large Yorkshire pudding, with currants sprinkled in one half just to add to the taste. In those days chicken was a luxury, generally only reserved for Christmas dinner.

Dad would ask me to play out at the front of the house in the morning, with some of my small lead Cowboy and Indian figures, and give him a shout when the 'Winkle Man' came around with his horse and cart and various items of seafood. Dad always bought one pint of winkles and a pint of shrimps in their shells. I only ever tasted a winkle once and immediately spat it out, as to me it tasted just like I was chewing on a grisly piece of a fishy tasting rubber band! Dad taught me how to extract the winkles out of their shells using a twisting corkscrew motion with a needle. You first removed the small disk covering the end of the winkle with the point of the needle, then inserted it into the flesh, twisted and pulled and out it came.

Dinner was served up with military precision at precisely 11.55am, just in time for the Two-Way Family Favourites wireless programme that started bang on noon. To the sound of, 'The time in Britain is twelve noon, in Germany it's one o'clock, but home and away it's time for Two-Way Family Favourites' we would then get stuck into some serious eating of the best meal of the week. Jean Metcalfe presented the British music requests and Cliff Michelmore did the same in Germany. I recall that the announcement went something like, 'This song is for Ronnie stationed in Hamburg at BFPO number etc, etc.' and they would then play the requested song for that British serviceman. Afters, was generally custard and jelly, custard and jam rolly-polly, or custard and apple pie. My preference was cold apple pie with evaporated milk poured over it.

The radio kept us quite entertained throughout the afternoon; there was Educating Archie, Hancocks Half Hour and also the Billy Cotton Band Show to look forward to, starting with Billy Cotton screaming out, 'Wakey-Wakey!' and followed with the usual weekly quip of, 'Who's that up there?' and then, 'Who's that down there in the glasses?' Oh, those magical radio days just sitting round that ugly big black bakelite wireless with hands cupped around your ears to magnify the sound and just letting your imagination run wild. Sunday night teatime had dad with a plate of bread and butter, sitting with his winkles lying in a dish just covered by a layer of vinegar, shelling his shrimps and washing it down with a pint of mild and bitter bought from the tap room at the Jubilee pub as he navigated his way through the Sunday newspapers. I amused myself playing games with lead soldiers, bagatelle, John Bull printing outfit, various board games or endeavouring to actually get some working models with my Meccano set.

We also had great variety street games to keep us amused in the 1950's. One favourite on the darker nights was 'knock down ginger', where you would simply knock on someone's door and run a safe distance to hide and watch the result. Then, immediately afterwards, we would see who drew the short straw to go up and knock again? Quite often people were wise to this and were just waiting behind the door for you to do it again. If caught, you were 'clumped' around the ear – there was no 'I know my rights' kind backchat in those days. This 'clump' would be even harder had you indulged in the more sinister version of 'knock down ginger' wherein black cotton was tied to the doorknocker and attached to a glass milk bottle placed on their windowsill. On opening the door the length of black cotton would pull the glass milk bottle right off the window sill and smash into small pieces right on their doorstep. Tin Tan Tommy was also a great favourite. This involved throwing a tin can up the street and one person ran after it whilst the others hid somewhere in the street. They would not look back, and upon reaching the tin can they would pick it up and then as quickly as possible run backwards to the point from where the tin can was thrown.

They would then leave the can, in the middle of the road, then walk off and search from the others. On finding someone they would run as fast as they could back to the can, then picking the can up would hammer it on the ground shouting "Tin Tan Tommy" followed by the person's name. This person would then be 'caught' and have to stand right next to the can while the person in charge of the can would replace it and search for the others. The persons caught would all stand 'captured' by the side of the tin can unless someone broke from their hiding place and was successful in reaching the can and kicking it up the street. At this point the captured kids would be set free and the whole process would start again. We also had great games of street cricket, using the telegraph pole at the corner of Westwood Road and Hanameel Street as the wicket. The streets were quite narrow and I am truly surprised that no residents complained, because we played it with a genuine solid leather cricket ball. Quite unbelievably, no windows were ever broken.

A common, rougher school playground game at the time was called 'Jimmy, Jimmy Knacker one-two-three.' This game was played with two teams of at least six kids in each team. One boy would stand with his back to the wall and the next member of his team would then bend forward, as if to play leap-frog, then placing both his hands either side of the boy against the wall he would place his head into the boys stomach. The next member of the team would then crouch forward, again in leap-frog mode, gripping the waist of the boy in front and placing his head against the boys buttocks and so on, until all the team members were in a straight line in the crouched leap-frog position. Then the opposing team members would take a long run and using leap-frog tactics, as they hit the very first crouched boy, would jump up and whacking the first boy on his back with the palms of their hands would launch themselves along the line of crouched boys aiming

Silvertown Life

Rathbone Street 1960 - Photo: Victor Elms (1911-1988), Lighterman of Canning Town

to land as close as possible to the boy with his back against the wall. The rest of the team would all then follow suit, again aiming to get as far down the chain as possible. When the last boy in your team had completed the mission and landed on the crouched chain of boys they would all sing loudly, 'Oi Jimmey Knacker 1-2-3, 1-2-3, 1-2-3, Oi Jimmey Knacker 1-2-3, 1-2-3, 1-2-3, Hooray!' The idea of the game was to place such a weight of boys at the weakest point of the line that the line of boys would collapse before the chant was finished. To cries of, 'Weak horses, Weak horses' your team had then won that test and it was now the other teams turn.

My favourite game by far was definitely 'British Bulldog', much rougher than any of the other playground games. This was definitely a game just for the boys and in the West Silvertown Primary School playground frequently ended in injuries. This was because the playground was littered throughout with tiny gravel like small sharp stones and also minute pieces of iron – small remnants of shrapnel from the War, we were told. If ever you fell over whilst just running then the graze on your knee invariably contained bits of the gritty playground surface. Well, Bulldog involved most of the boys in the last two years of the school standing at one end of the playground with just one boy in the middle. The boy in the middle would shout out 'Bulldog!' and all the boys would then run past him, to the opposite end of the playground. The idea of the game was for the boy in the middle to catch hold of just one boy and lift him clear off the ground shouting 'Bulldog!' Then the two of them would stand in the middle, shout, 'Bulldog!' and then the whole procedure would be repeated again. It got very, very rough when just the strongest last few boys were left and the mob, having finally caught them tossed them in the air, sometimes just leaving them to fall on the rough playground surface.

6

Life in the Children's Homes

Due to over crowding, poor diet and the subsequent bad health quite a few kids were sent to children's convalescent homes. I vividly recall some of my convalescent experiences. They started in 1949 when I was 4½ years of age. I am told that it was a combination of over crowding in the house and me being 'highly strung'. My first convalescent home was the well-known 'Sunshine Home' at Shoeburyness, in Essex. It must have been summertime, because I recall that we would all walk to the beach in a group and play alongside the beach huts. I remember that while I was picking up seashells on the beach a family started talking to me and asked me to stand still so they could take a photograph of me. I must have been bright enough to know my home address, because the photo was sent direct to my mum. Mum was then daft enough to send it on to me, because I recall that while playing in the grounds of the home, near the entrance, I saw Mr Kirby from Boxley Street walk up to the door of the home and deliver a parcel. One of the staff then gave me a couple of small toys, one of which was a small cap bomb that gave me hours of fun, and also the photograph of me standing on the beach. By the following day I had lost it!

The staff in children's homes could be quite cruel. One boy, just a little older than me, played up from time to time. I used to be friendly with him because he slept in the next bed to me in our dormitory. One day he had got hold of a box of matches, which terrified me. We both walked round to the back of the Sunshine Home where there was a haystack. He set fire to it and all hell broke loose. When the staff caught up with him he struggled like mad, kicking all and sundry and ended up being put into some kind of harness in which his arms were folded across the front of his body and tied around his back, some sort of straight-jacket. He was then tossed, struggling into a high-sided cot with drop-down bars and the door slammed shut. While he was trussed up we were all singing 'Horsey, Horsey, don't you stop, just let your feet go clipperty clop' in the main hall and my mind was constantly on him all trussed up in the dormitory.

We sat at long tables and on long wooden forms in the dining hall and I remember the very first time I ever ate what I now believe was plaice. I had never seen this type of boiled fish before and was horrified to see a dark slimy skin with coloured spots, which were orange colour. To me it looked just like a real fish lying on the plate and it was served with mashed potatoes and peas. I just could not bring myself to eat it. I was the only one left in the hall and an impatient female member of staff came up and shouted at me, demanding that I eat it. I just couldn't. By now the meal was well cold, nevertheless, she scooped up a portion of the fish, spotted skin as well, and forced it into my mouth. Again I was shouted at and my nose was held as I was ordered to swallow. I swallowed and my nose was released. I was so traumatised by what had happened that I vomited the whole lot up over the plate.

I thought for one brief moment that would be the end of it. Unfortunately for me, that was not to be. The lady shouted, "Eat it!" and I said, through my tears "I've been sick." She replied, "Then you'll eat that as well, or you'll stay here 'til you do." She mashed the whole thing up, then departed and left me for what seemed like ages. She returned, walked over to me, looked at the plate of cold fish, mash and vomit and again shouted, "Eat it!" I cried, but knew that I must submit to her demands, so I got on and ate the vomit-covered meal.

I had eaten most of it by the time she had returned and again crying I said, "I can't eat any more." She pulled the plate off the table and just walked away. I got up and went to join the other children in the main hall. Children are remarkably resilient and seem to adjust to any situation. By the following day the incident, although imbedded in my subconscious mind, was on the surface forgotten and I got on with my life in the home. Although, I did many years later as an adult, wonder what type of person could torment a child less than five years of age in such a cruel way. What difference did it make to her that I did not like that particular meal and why did she not just take it away?

Later on in the home the matron and two strangers waked me in the night. I was then bundled into an ambulance, which I found rather confusing and once in the ambulance I started to cry. The nurse accompanying me to the hospital was very sympathetic and calmed me down. I was then placed into a single bedded room and fell asleep. I stayed in bed all the next day and remember that in the evening the sister tried to give me an injection. I recall the struggle and I was held down screaming, as I was frightened of having the injection. The following night I was asleep as the sister gave me the injection, which woke me as the needle went into my arm. Being half-asleep I did not put up a struggle or make a great deal of fuss, so the sister gave me a square of chocolate. The following night the sister must have thought that all would be well again, but I was wide-awake and made the usual fuss. I recall that she was furious and gave me a good telling off afterwards and a smack on the face with her hand. The reason I was in hospital was suspected scarlet fever, but I think this proved to be untrue. Mum and dad came into my room on one occasion and I thought at that point that I was going home, but of course I wasn't, which made me even more distressed. Eventually I was returned to the Sunshine Home and then, back home to Silvertown.

The second home I went to must have been just after Christmas 1949. I clearly recall that all the Christmas decorations were still up, and there was a very large real pine Christmas tree in a huge room. I was initially quite apprehensive and sad at being away from my familiar surroundings. However, it did not take me long to settle into this wonderful place. I was running around the huge room and playing around the Christmas tree. I also recall the fun I had with one of the staff, a tall, constantly smiling blonde woman. I remember looking into her face and shouting, "You are a werewolf." I can still see the surprise on her face now. Looking back, as I ran away, I saw her laughing and shouting to another member of staff "He's just called me a werewolf."

I have absolutely no idea how I had any knowledge of werewolves at that young age. I think that had I stayed there forever I would quickly have become institutionalised and forgotten my family in Silvertown. On 27th January 1950 I received a Birthday card from mum and dad, with a large figure 5 on the front. I remember sitting alone at a table and staring at it for quite some time and thinking about mum and dad. I really did have a great time at this home; making friends with a black boy called Batush Arthur Warrior. When suddenly, one day, I was told that I was going home I got quite excited, but at the same time felt rather upset at finally having to leave the home.

I remember with absolute clarity what was for me a particularly poignant moment just before leaving when, dressed in my topcoat, I realised that before getting on the coach I needed a trip to the toilet. As I walked into the toilet coincidentally my friend Batush was standing at the urinal about to have a pee. I stood next to him fiddled under my coat and started to pee – not a word was said and it seemed to go on for ages. Suddenly Batush, without turning to look at me, said "Goodbye Stanley Dyson." Without looking back I replied "Goodbye Batush Arthur Warrior" and ran out of the toilet with tears streaming down my face. I am sure that we both knew inside that we would never see each other again.

It was not until I was in my early forties that I discovered the home was in Herne Bay, Kent. Walking along the sea front esplanade I came to an area with a large grass covered hill between the seafront and main road above, with a distinctive zig-zag footpath connecting the two areas. This was familiar to me and on looking in the local Herne Bay library I discovered that there had been a children's home called 'Batesholme' at a point just above the winding footpath. I was disappointed that the home had been demolished a few years earlier as I would love to have had a nostalgic walkabout to see if any other hidden memories re-surfaced. I must have lost all sense of time whilst in these homes because I thought I had been there for just a couple of weeks. I see from looking at entries in West Silvertown Primary School register that I was re-admitted to the school on 24th April 1950, so given that I was there just after Christmas and had my 5th Birthday in the home in January then I had been there for months. It really didn't matter to me because I loved the place. We had plenty of exercise walking along the seafront every day, hence the familiar winding footpath, and my dormitory, shared with about six other boys, looked straight out across the estuary. I enjoyed waking up to the sea view and seeing the boats on the horizon. In fact, I had a brief problem settling back into our dingy house in Westwood Road again. I remember feeling a bit strange at being in the company of mum again and feeling distinctly claustrophobic, as the small living room seemed to be closing in on me. In all those months I had become used to very large rooms and open spaces

The next children's home I stayed at was in Broadstairs, Kent in late October or early November 1951. I know that it was the approximate time because after being there a short time we celebrated Guy Fawkes with a bonfire in the large brick walled back garden. I was just about the youngest boy in that large detached residence. The home was situated next to a farm that we used to walk by on our way to the beach. After passing the farm we would take a sharp right turn and walk down a long, very narrow path that had trees and dense bushes on either side of it. On exiting the path we would cross a road and there was the beach. I also remember lining up with the other kids in the hallway of the home on 5th November, waiting to walk into the back garden for the bonfire and fireworks. I was tapped on the shoulder from behind by one of the older boys and as I turned he thrust his finger into my mouth. It went right back to the start of my throat and made me gag a bit. As my throat closed and I did an involuntary swallow I was conscious of something in my mouth. I moved it forward onto my tongue and spit it into my hand. It was a huge bogey he had picked from his nose. I can still taste it now! The other kids thought it was hilarious and as I tried to protest, one of the staff came up and said that if I didn't stop the commotion I would go straight upstairs to bed, instead of seeing the fireworks. This was a very religious home, because we were always being read bible stories and regularly indulged in hymn singing. From records in the school register I see that I returned to West Silvertown school life on 22nd November 1951.

In 1981 I went for the very first time, I thought, to a Kent seaside resort called Broadstairs. When I saw the curve of the sandy beach from the small pier a sort of déjà vu came over me. I tried like mad to think why the place looked so familiar. Then a short time later, while walking through the town streets, many things looked familiar. Then I had a sort of premonition of a Church being just around the corner. I then told my wife that if there was a church just around the corner I might well have lived in this area before. I had always been fascinated with the idea of reincarnation and thought that I was on the threshold of something big.

We turned the corner and there was the church, just as I had imagined, although it was slightly different. Where in my minds eye I had seen the roadside sloping, without a break, up to the church, now there was a small wall in the way. Also, the church did not have the same spire as I had previously imagined and I was looking at it from the wrong angle. I began walking towards the correct viewpoint outside a small parade of old shops. When I arrived at the corner shop it all came flooding back. Suddenly, I was back waiting outside a sweet shop with other kids and looking towards a man struggling to push a large wheeled market stall up the slope towards the church. He was wearing a cloth cap and had a large handlebar moustache, looking quite unbelievably the double of my Granddad. Then I knew that this was the place where I had stayed as a kid, in one of the children's homes. I thought that I must find the place where I had stayed and rushed back to the beach, hoping that I could find the narrow pathway to the farm and then the children's home. Once I was on the beach another memory came flooding back of a small boy sitting on a sandy beach with other kids clutching a large used rocket he had found, as a remnant from one of last nights 5th November firework display. An adult said sternly, "Throw that away!" Instead I buried it in the sand and clearly recall my thoughts at the time, that I would retrieve it later.

Finding the elusive narrow path had now become a quest. I tried backtracking from the beach and crossing the road and suddenly there was the path. It was unchanged, just as I remembered it. It ran alongside the local High School or College. I was so excited as I got to the end of the familiar path, as I knew that there was a left-hand turn, then the farm and finally the children's home. As I exited the path, there in front of me was a huge housing estate. The trail had become cold and nothing was familiar anymore. I immediately went to the local studies library and made enquiries. Yes, there was a farm and a children's home, but that was all demolished years ago to make way for the housing estate. What about the church then and the sweet shop? I was a bit puzzled because in my mind there should have been a sweet shop on the corner, not a DIY shop. The librarian came back with photographs of the old church as it used to look before the small wall was built and yes, it was just as I remembered it. By looking at old records the librarian also established that the DIY shop was a sweet shop back in the 1950's. Despite my disappointment at not seeing things as they were previously, I had really enjoyed my day and revived and relived long forgotten memories.

I believe that the fourth and final home I stayed in was in summer 1952, when I was seven. I have no idea where the home was other than it was a very large detached residence with a prefabricated annex, used as a separate dormitory. It was surrounded by woodland, with lots of pine tree's and there was an 'out of bounds' area about 250 yards into the woods, as this was the border of a nearby dog kennel business. Most of the time you could hear the barking of dogs in the distance. There was quite a lot of 'roughing up' amongst the boys in residence. Sometimes playful, other times serious and the staff were very strict and swift to discipline any kind of boisterous activities. As I was one of the youngest in the group I was picked on from time to time. Initially, I was passed into the care of one of the older boys and slept in the prefabricated annex. There was quite a lot of boisterous activity, pillow fights and wrestling around, until the very strict male master would enter the building, have a loud shout up and discipline the senior boys. One night, just as we were going to bed, one of the senior boys gave me a mug of water to drink. It was warm and tasted rather odd. I gave it back to him saying that I did not like the taste, at which point they all laughed and he shouted, "Yes, we all pissed in it!" I told the senior master and was then moved into the main residence.

One night one of the older, more disruptive boys was tormenting and bullying the boy in the next bed, making quite a commotion. The strictest of the masters shouted up "Whose making all that noise?" and the disruptive boy shouted back "Its Dyson, sir." The master shouted up the stairs, 'Dyson, come down here!' I did not respond, but just buried myself deep beneath my blanket, frightened of what may happen and hoping it would all just go away. He called out again, 'Dyson, down here!' Again, no response from me, and with that the master bounded up the stairs and pulled me out of the bed by grabbing my pyjamas at the shoulder and dragged me down stairs. Although I was quite frightened and very near to tears I protested my innocence, but to no avail, and I made a conscious decision not to snitch, as I knew that the disruptive boy would certainly get me later. He opened the kitchen door and threw me into the darkness of the room. He shouted, "You stay there and don't touch that light!" The whole house was dark and I found it very frightening standing alone looking through the kitchen window into the darkness of the woods outside. I was there for hours, if not the whole night; I cannot quite recall now, but I know I did drop off to sleep for a short period just lying on the floor. I was not too displeased to leave that residence.

7

First taste of corporal punishment

One popular past time for many of us was the joy of climbing onto our school roof. The school was huge and once on the roof there was a labyrinth of gully's and passages to walk around. You could shin up one lead covered rain gully, between the roof slates, and then carefully ease yourself down the other side and be on a completely different part of the school roof. You had to carefully ease yourself down the other side because the roof gradient was so steep that if you rushed there was a danger of slipping right off the end of the roof and serious injury, if not death. The roof areas were also great for games of hide and seek. It was quite an effort getting on the school roof in the first place, because first you had to shin up a double story height of drainpipe. There were two alternative easier ways by climbing up the single story drain pipe, but the downside of that was you were in full view of the caretaker, Harry Webster's, school house window. If he saw you would be for it! He would not shin up the drainpipe, but he was skilled in stealthily using his ladder and jumping out on you. He caught Richie Coke and me once, just after Richie had decided that he couldn't wait to get home to the toilet so did it on the roof. Harry was furious and made Richie clear it all up. We certainly suffered in school the following day after being hauled in front of the Head Mistress, who made the comment, 'I'm really surprised at you Stanley.' Although it was a very dangerous place to play, the only serious school roof accident I can recall was when Roy Walker endeavoured to walk across one of the glass skylight in his hob nailed boots. He went straight through the skylight leaving him with a very nasty cut down his leg that required many stitches.

In May 1953 we had an addition to our family, when my brother, John Edward, was born. I was still progressing through my primary school life and was very relieved when I left Mr Davies's class and went into the final primary school years with the jovial Mr O'Sullivan. He was quite swarthy and of Irish descent, always smiling, with a mop of dark brown hair and very ruddy cheeks. I recall these years with fondness, because Mr O'Sullivan certainly seemed to bring the best out of all of us all. He was a great one for getting over the essential reading, writing, spelling and arithmetic that we would all need for the essential 11-plus examinations. He really did interact well with our class and was well liked. He encourage us to do presentations in a roundabout way by getting us to stand in front of the class and tell stories, something I excelled at!

The only time I fell foul of Mr O'Sullivan was my first year in his class when I made a remark about another girl in front of the whole class. She could not understand the work he wanted her to do, so she burst into tears. I shouted out "Was that the hooter?" Which made her cry even louder. He was furious! He asked Michael Taylor to find the cane in his drawer. I couldn't believe it! Caned, for just a comment? I was hoping that Michael wouldn't find it, but no such luck. This was quite humiliating for me, not to mention frightening, as I had never been caned before in my life. He called me out to the front of the class and made me hold my hand out. There was a swish, as the cane came down across my hand. I don't think it even hurt that much, but I felt quite humiliated, as this had been a spectacle for the rest of the class. Fortunately it all happened just before 'playtime' and gave me the opportunity to 'get my own back.' All the kids crowded around me asking to see the damage and I felt quite good at being the centre of attention by showing them the red welt across my hand. The last person to see the red welt was Michael Taylor, from 17 Westwood Road, and I said to him "I'm off now. I'm running away from school."

He shouted, "Where are you going?" I was bit nervous at the possibility of not being found, so as I ran out of the school gates I shouted back "To the camp."

Well, we had three different camps, one in the bushes by the bandstand in Lyle Park, another next to the dock fence by Ranks Cottages, at the end of Evelyn Road, but that was far too close to the school. I ran to my favourite camp down North Woolwich Road, past the Ram Public House, up the steps by the Royal Victoria Docks rail entrance and onto the viaduct. Then across the Tidal Basin causeway that joins Victoria Dock to the Thames and down the steps of the viaduct to the triangular area of grass immediately opposite that sloped to the lower part of North Woolwich Road and the start of Dock Road. This triangular area ran adjacent to the steps by the side of the viaduct and was generally known as 'the arches' in Dock Road where people used to shelter from the German aerial attacks during the bombing in the Second World War.

After sitting in the clump of bushes, by the iron fence at the top of the grass verge, for what seemed an eternity, Michael Taylor finally arrived. He said that he had told Mr O'Sullivan that I had run away from school and that he knew where to find me. He wanted to march me back, but I wasn't having any of that, so we agreed on him going back to the school and telling them I was on my way. I stopped on the debri opposite our house in Westwood Road. The debri was now called 'the iron field' because huge rusty girders had been stacked everywhere. I choose to hide amongst these and saw my mum coming from the direction of the school. Unfortunately, before I popped my head down she also saw me! Mum called me across the road in her usual annoyed manner, 'Get over here my boy!' she shouted. After standing at the street door for some considerable time, initially pointing her fingers and continually shouting, "Get indoors!" and me pleading not to be hit, she mellowed a bit and agreed there would be no 'good hiding' as long as I came indoors quickly. That promise was broken the moment I passed through our front door and, ducking low to avoid mums swinging right hand slap, I ran down the passage into the living room and dived right under the dining room table. As usual, out came the yard broom and after absorbing several painful pokes, out I scurried out for further punishment.

8

First Love and Bradfield Road adventures

I really enjoyed the 1950's. Every day seemed a sunny day, there was always something happening to keep us occupied and we had lots of laughs. One funny incident that sticks in my mind happened close to Guy Fawkes Night, just before the Batterbee's were re-housed. It was customary for us to build a guy and stand outside the Jubilee Pub, the shops, factories or the dock entrance gates asking adults for a 'penny for the guy'. This aways helped with our fireworks fund. The Batterbee's built a terrific lifelike guy. One evening Bridget Batterbee's sister-in-law, Bella, knocked at our front door asking for Bridgette. As Bridgette wasn't in Bella said that she would sit at the very top of the stairs and wait for her to return. On entering the house Bridgette looked up the stairs, squinted her eyes and said to my mum "Look where they've left that bleeding guy." Bella replied, "Thanks to you Bridgette, it's me!"

One of the early 1950's most exciting places to be was at the wooden steps that led down to the River Thames at the end of Bradfield Road. We used to call the area 'The Bank'. When the tide was out used to turn left at the bottom of the steps and walk the distance along the riverbank to the frontage at Lyle Park. In places the mud was at least one foot deep and literally sucked your shoes off. We used to do it bare feet carrying our shoes and it took ages to get the polluted black mud off our feet. There was no fear of being 'taken away' by strangers in those days. In 1959 I remember going on a small Dutch steamship that was moored right alongside the river steps and chatting to the young crew. One of them was called 'Yacob', which I now know was Jacob. They gave us a tour of the ship and offered some soft drinks. They were clearly very bored moored up at the end of Bradfield Road and asked where there was some entertainment and fun. I took them to the funfair at Beckton Park. We walked all the way from Silvertown, across the Canning Town Viaduct, and they complained about the distance. It didn't bother me because I always walked everywhere. They were a really friendly bunch of Seamen, probably in their early twenties and they paid for all our rides on the dodgems and roundabouts. I was puzzled why they were so obsessed with chatting up the English girls rather than enjoying all the rides.

I remember my very first 'love' and how heartbroken I was when she left me, after all of a few hours – and we didn't even speak! I would have been about 8 or 9 years of age at the time. There was a 'big do' over Lyle Park with the Dagenham Girl Pipers in attendance and I have no idea what it was all about. There was also a troop of Brownies from either Becontree, or Beaconsfield, and when I saw one of them it was 'love at first sight'. I don't think she had even noticed me. I sort of 'stalked' her, and was absolutely fascinated by her. I asked someone to find out her name, maybe it was one of her friends, and I was told that her name was Erica Woods. On being pointed out to her, and being told of my interest, she smiled at me. I tingled all over and nearly died of embarrassment. Then, as quick as they had arrived they were gone. I was heartbroken and walked over to 'fatty Patient's' gangs camp, which was situated just outside Lyle Park, on the debri between Bradfield and Knights Roads. The camp was just by the large tree, with the long rope attached to one of the thick branches that we all used as a swing. It must have been by the remnants of a bomb crater because there was quite a slope by the side of the tree and you could swing out a long way. I sat in the branch-covered camp and cried my eyes out at the departure of Erica and I was so distraught that I did not think I would survive the day.

I tried to join 'fatty' Patient's gang once. His real name was Brian Patient and he did not seem to mind being referred to as 'fatty', although looking back he did not seem that fat to me. The 'gang' was all standing around the tree swing at the time I 'applied' for membership. I recall just walking up and asking, "Can I join fatty Patient's gang?" I wasn't even sure of which one of them was fatty Patient. I do recall that as they were between four or five years older than me my request was met with some amusement. However, I was quite serious and they had a talk about it and said they would give some tests. One of the tests was hanging onto the rope swing for dear life as they pushed me in every conceivable direction, after they had twisted the rope sufficiently to ensure that I spun vigorously. Another test was carrying very long and heavy items, possibly planks of wood, up the slope towards the tree swing. I thought that I passed all the tests, but they did not let me join. I believe that the tests were halted when Bonny Murphy, the Irish lady who lived in the last house at the very edge of the Knights Road side of the debri, shouted over her garden fence about all the noise we were making. Bonny Murphy was quite a local character. Sometimes Bonny used to take a live eel in a bucket of water for a walk along the streets. She would often shout out a very loud, 'Clear-Off' over her back fence at any kids who were engaged in various battles or other debri game activities by the tree swing.

At the far end of Knights Road, between the Bonny Murphy's house and the bombed debri area was the very last remaining house, number 52, where the Hill family lived. Albert Hill was the father, whose sister Edith Hill, was married to Charlie Eagland from 23 Westwood Road. Ellen Hill was the mother and the boys were Michael Hill, a year older than me, also Jeffrey Hill, slightly younger than me. Although there was no boundary fence to their garden I believe that they looked upon quite an area of the debri as 'their' territory. I did get on quite well with the Hills and frequently ended up playing in their huge back yard. Part of the area immediately to the side of the back yard was surrounded by a very small wall and was part of John Knights soap factory property. This concrete area appeared to be almost always covered in water. I recall that in the course of playing with Michael Hill I discovered that his mother gave him the same gooey cod liver oil and malt mixture that I was given by my mother. I think that it was something to do with the prevention of rickets. In those day's National dried milk and National orange juice was also the order of the day for us kids. I absolutely loved the sharp and distinctive taste of the concentrated National orange juice, which had to be diluted with water, and it certainly beats any kind of orange juice concentrate that is in circulation these days. I would dearly love to taste the sharpness of that drink again today. There was a very large tree about six feet from the water logged walled area and one day I had climbed it and was sitting on one of the large branches, about ten feet above the ground, when I slipped. I landed right on the top of my head and was unconscious for a minute or two. I remember 'coming round' with a very sore head and stiff neck with Michael looking at me very puzzled and Ellen Hill running up the yard towards me. I was quite lucky to have survived what must have been about a ten-foot fall directly onto my head, but fortunately for me it was on part of the field and not the concrete flooded area just three feet away.

9

Friendly Vicars and runaways caught in the act.

In the mid 1950's many of us were in the St Barnabus Church choir. This must have been just after the Vicar Peter May had left the Parish. My Nan, Alice Guinee, was quite upset at Peter May's departure as she had a lot of involvement in St Barnabus Church matters, along with her Scottish friend Martha Smith, who lived in the prestigious Lyles houses at 24 Evelyn Road. I forget the name of the Vicar that replaced Peter May but it was during this period that I joined the choir. Listening to mum it appeared that it was the consensus of opinion amongst the adults that he was a bit too friendly and 'touchy, touchy' with the boys in the choir. Nevertheless, I stayed in the choir until such time as I missed choir practice because of illness and the vicar subsequently visited our house to see me. He was sitting at the table in our middle living room on the chair immediately in front of the door, speaking to my mum. He picked me up and sat me on his lap, continuing to speak to mum. Inadvertently, (hopefully) his hand, that was periodically patting my thighs, moved across the top of my legs and patted my groin area. For mum, that was it! I never did return to the choir during his period of residency.

Another Vicar, who we all, despite being Church of England Protestants, had to address as 'Father' replaced him. I then became re-associated with the Church and the choir. As I am discussing matters of the church, leaping forward in time somewhat to the age of around twelve to thirteen years of age, it became clear that I was a bit different to the other kids my age. For instance, dissatisfied with the nominal 'bang' that you got from commercial fireworks I used to make my own. They were almost miniature bombs! Talk about 'light the blue touch paper and retire to a safe distance', with my fireworks you had to 'leg it' and hide behind a brick wall! They really did go with a bang. I always made my own gunpowder using flowers of sulphur, saltpetre and charcoal. In one of my early experiments in the kitchen at Westwood Road, after burning sulphur on the gas stove we all had to evacuate the house to escape the acrid fumes. I was also very much into reading books about flying saucers, extra terrestrial visits, death and the afterlife and occultism. I had already read all the Dennis Wheatly novels on black magic and was currently reading a non-fiction book called 'The Third Eye' by the author T. Lobsang Rampa and H. P. Blavatsky's 'The Secret Doctrine'.

Anyway, getting back to the church, one evening the Vicar asked me to call into his residential area situated right at the side of the Church. On entering his residence I was somewhat surprised to see that he was only wearing a purple dressing gown and slippers. We went to his personal living quarters and he sat down in an armchair, crossing his legs and inviting me to sit opposite. At this point his dressing gown fell open revealing his bare legs, right up past his thighs. I nervously started talking to him about Lobsang Rampa's book 'The Third Eye' and then got onto Dennis Wheatley's book, 'The Devil Rides Out'. I recall asking him what the translation of the Latin words 'Fundamenta ejus in montibus sanctis,' (not sure about the spelling here because it was a long time ago) that appeared in the book meant. He replied, 'That means, I think Stanley, The Foundations of God are in Sacred Mountains.' I recall almost word for word what he said next, namely "Stanley, you're not like the other boy's and I know I can speak to you directly. I want you to know that if you have any problems, or worries about anything, like masturbation, then you can always come and speak to me about it." That was it for me! I may of course have completely misread his intentions, but what with him sitting there in his purple robe, with nothing visible underneath and wide open past his thighs, and asking me questions about masturbation - I was out of there like a rat up a drainpipe! I did not become further involved in church matters after this date.

Also, around this period there was another strange sexually related incident that happened to me inside of Canning Town's Imperial cinema. Around the age of 11 or 12-years of age I stopped going to evening cinema with dad and just went alone. Generally this was for the 'U' certificate films, because if it was an 'A' certificate film at my age you were denied admission unless you were accompanied by an adult. Sometimes, if it were an 'A' certificate film I fancied seeing, I would wait outside the cinema and pester the adults by asking, 'Can you take me into the pictures please mister?' In the light of modern day awareness, as a young kid this was quite a dangerous thing to do. Anyway, on one particular visit I was sitting in my seat watching the film and I became aware of a strange sensation in the area of my groin. It was almost as if I had developed a pulse in that area. It was a regular beat, like a very light tapping or patting sensation. Slowly, I bent my head down slightly and lowered my eyes – to my horror there was a hand hovering over my groin with the fingers just patting lightly away! I looked sharply to my left, at which point the hand was swiftly whisked away. I recognised the person as a fairly scruffy and dishevelled local street trader. I quickly jumped up and exited that row of seats just to find somewhere else to sit. As I looked back I saw the figure of a man disappearing out of the left hand side exit doors of the cinema and looking back at where I was previously seated the 'groin patter' had vanished. I didn't let this minor 'interference' distract me from enjoying the rest of the film, but I made a mental note to give the perpetrator a very wide berth at any future date. I mentioned both the incident and the perpetrator to another friend, who also knew the man and his family. He advised me to keep very quiet about the incident because he said the mans son, who was slightly older than me, was a complete 'nutter' and would most certainly beat me up if the story got back to him. Needless to say, I took his good advice and never mentioned it to anyone else.

Whizzing back again to 1956, this was my last year in Mr O'Sullivans class and primary school. By then I had got quite a reputation as a

The Dyson family 1956

'storyteller'. We had by now taken our 11-plus examinations to see who would go to Grammar or Technical Schools and who would go to Secondary Modern Schools. Given that the exams were now behind us Mr O'Sullivan frequently allowed the class to choose whom they wanted to stand at the front and tell the class a story. I was chosen nearly every time, to relate my Tom, Dick and Harry stories. Tom, Dick and Harry got into all sorts of adventures in haunted houses, horror stories, crime detection and kidnapping and the class loved them. Unfortunately, Mr O'Sullivan probably had a low boredom threshold and 'banned' me for a period, 'to give others the chance', he said. I was fortunate enough to have scraped through the 11-plus examinations and I chose South West Ham Technical School at the Barking Road, Canning Town for my secondary education.

In 1955 we had the final addition to our family on 17th December when my brother, Roger George, was born. Mid 1950's Silvertown was a very sociable and people orientated area in which to live. There was not the distraction of television and video games like today. The summer months seemed exceedingly hot, to the point that the tarmacadum covering the streets used to actually bubble under the heat. Adults used to sit on the window ledges or copings outside of their houses until late into the summer evenings passing the time and chatting to neighbours and residents from nearby streets who were just passing by. This was a very close-knit area with no fears about burglary, which did not really exist at all. In fact, many of the houses had their front doors 'on the string' which meant that you just stuffed your hand through their letter box and felt about a bit, until you located a piece of string that was just hanging down. The string was attached to the door latch and by just pulling the string through the letterbox and giving it a tug you opened their street door.

It was around this period in the mid 1950's that I suddenly became more interested in the female of the species. It is almost as if the minute hand on some biological clock had just clicked onto 'sex'. I recall that I was with Richie Coke, whose house in Eastwood Road backed onto our house in Westwood Road. We met each other whilst walking to the field at the end of Boxley Street, opposite our school, where a small fun fair had arrived. On arriving at the fair we sort of bumped into Louisa and Jeanie and after a brief exchange of greetings we all decided that it would be a good idea to walk across Evelyn Road to the dock fence at the end of Ranks Cottages in order to satisfy our sexual curiosity. In many ways it was quite innocent sexual exploration. I was with Louisa and Richie was with Jeanie. We all lay in the dip by the edge of the Dock fence and long grass hid us from anyone passing by in Evelyn Road. We had a couple of brief kisses and the girls then obliged by lifting up their dresses and pulling down their knickers. Richie and me pulled down our trousers and we all had a good look at each other. I was lying down with Louisa and Ritchie was with Jeanie. I think there may also have been some exploratory touching, at which point it was all spoiled by the sound of voices coming towards us. It was Louisa's older sister Lilly and another girl. Clearly they had not actually seen us, but were just scouring the vicinity calling out Louisa's name. At this point the two girls panicked, jumped up and still trying to hoist their knickers up ran away.

Richie also jumped up and quickly followed Jeanie and Louisa. They were vigorously all pursued and caught by Louisa's outraged older sister. I kept very low in the grass dip and hugging the dock fence, I crawled along on my stomach towards the last house in Ranks Cottages, where Charlie Flemwell parked his black London taxi. I crawled underneath the taxi and watched the two older girls searching along the dock fence amongst the long grass. I felt quite safe and thought I was completely off the hook, but one of them suddenly said "What about under the taxi?" They came towards me and looked under the taxi. I was caught! Louisa's older sister, Lilly said, "Come out Dyson, you've been having 'digs' with Louisa, haven't you?" I crawled out and said "No." Lily replied, "Yes you have, you've been having a 'do' and I am going round to tell your Mum." I realised that Richie must have 'shopped' me to Louisa's older sister, but I doubted that she would actually knock on my door and tell my mum. How wrong I was! I stood with Ritchie at the corner of Evelyn Road and Westwood Road, watching them walk towards my house. They disappeared into my doorway. I thought that maybe they were just standing there to make me think they were knocking. It seemed like ages had past, then suddenly, like a whirlwind, mum swept out of the house with her black mackintosh flapping behind her. With her black coat puffed out in the wind, she looked just like Batman on a mission, with Lily and friend running close behind her.

I said to Richie, "That's it, I'm running away from home, are you coming?" Richie nodded and we both ran back down Evelyn Road, past the 'leccie' (electricity sub-station) on the corner of Boxley Street to the fun fair. Just to ensure that we were found, I briefly stopped and told a couple of the kids that we were running away from home because we got caught having 'a do' with the girls at the dock fence, albeit that I wasn't even quite sure what 'a do' was at that particular time. I also said don't tell any one that we were running away to 'Itchycoo Park', the very large bombed site and waste ground adjacent to the Graving Dock Tavern. This area was previously known as Silvertown Recreational Park, but was subsequently destroyed by German bombing in World War 2. We 'legged' it like mad along the dock fence, past Gulf Oil, Silcocks and The Silvertown Tarmacadum Company to the waste ground at the side of the Graving Dock entrance gates. I do recall being surprised that we had got that far and no one had chased after us.

When we got to the area at the back of the Graving Dock Tavern pub I immediately climbed up the gradient of the concrete ridge that supported the dock fence to the full height of about ten feet. After about half-hour I got bored of clinging on for dear life to the dock fence and, still surprised that no one had pursued us, climbed down again. Richie and me were starting to get bored, so we chased the chickens that had come from out of the broken fence at the back of the Graving Dock Tavern around the fields for a bit. This caused quite a commotion, to the point that a couple of gypsy boys, about our age, appeared from out of the bushes. Richie and I spoke to them and told them that we had run away from home, although we did not tell them why. They seemed quite dismayed. They appeared to be quite religious and we then asked them if we could stay with them. They went away and asked their parents, who were in a caravan at the very back of the waste ground. Unsurprisingly, the answer was no, but the boys seemed very curious and almost in awe of us. From memory we both played up to it and there was a lot of bravado. In fact, enjoying the infamy, I had almost forgotten that by now some hours had elapsed since we made a run for it.

Suddenly, we heard a car approaching and looking into the direction of the sound we saw a black saloon car screech to a halt about 100 yards away. Two men I didn't immediately recognise jumped out. I still wasn't sure if they were searching for us, then out came 'Batwoman', with her black cloak still flapping – 'mum' I thought and shouted, "Lets run for it!" We both ran through the bushes together, with the men in hot pursuit. We ran around to the North Woolwich Road side of the Graving Dock Tavern and I said, "Lets run into the railway goods yard", which was across the road alongside Thomas W Ward's factory.

As we ran across the North Woolwich Road I had hoped that we could have lost our pursuers amongst all the railway wagons parked alongside Thomas W Wards. I could hear the sound of swift feet behind me and as I tried to jump across the railway lines a hand grabbed my collar and I was caught! I fell to the ground, between the railway lines. I looked up and saw that it was one of the very much older Smith brothers from 18 Knights Road. It was either Allan or Kenny Smith. Mum was very friendly with the Smiths and used to visit their house a couple of times a week. As I was lying on the ground I saw a large rusty nail, which I picked up and pressed against my neck and said, "If you don't let me go I'll dig it right in." "Go on then." He said, looking down at me, completely unconcerned. I had played my final card and lost, so I just dropped the nail. He yanked me up and pulled across the road to the car. Batwoman, sticking her head through the open passenger car window hissed through closed teeth, "Just wait until I get you home my boy." Mum sat in the front of the car and I sat on her lap. Not a further word was spoken to me, but she was full of thanks and praise to the driver. Suddenly, the back door of the car flew open and Richie was forced in. He was kicking and fighting like mad. I don't think he knew any of his captors, as mum had engineered the lot. They had to open the offside passenger window otherwise Richies feet would have smashed the rear windscreen. He continued to struggle all the way home.

As soon as the car stopped I ran indoors and straight upstairs to the back room at the top of the stairs, Kathy's bedroom, as I knew it had a small bolt on it. Strange that it had a bolt on it because there was no such thing as 'security' in those days. Everybody was poor, in varying degrees, and in any case most houses were on the 'latch'. All you had to do was put your hand through the letterbox, locate the piece of string that was attached to the door lock, pull it and the door opened. I closed the door, turned the lock and stuck my ear to the bedroom door. I couldn't believe it, dad didn't even know, as I could hear mum telling him what had happened. Suddenly dad came bounding up the stairs and unsuccessfully tried to open the door. "Open the door!" He shouted. "No." I said, "You'll hit me." Dad replied, "If you don't open the door I'll hit you!" He banged on the door very hard. I knew that he could easily break the fragile bolt, so I gave in and opened the door. Dad looked furious. "What have you done?" he demanded. I did my best to explain how we got caught after playing with the girls. "What did you do to the girls then?" he asked. I said, trying to play it all down as much as possible "I just pulled down their drawers." Dad said, "Did they let you?" I replied, "Yes, they did." "Right", said dad "don't do it again." And walked back down the stairs. That was it. What an anticlimax! I really felt that I had been let off the hook, but I must say that I can never ever remember my dad ever hitting me; but mum, well that's another story.

The following day a row erupted between Richies mum and my mum. Richies mum was hanging out of the upstairs window at the back of her house and my mum was in our back yard. I can distinctly recall the words "You keep your Stanley away from my Richie." And mums reply "Yes, and you can keep your Richie away from my Stanley." That was the end of the matter, nearly. The following day Richie and me bathed in the glory of the stories of our small sexual adventure, the discovery, and subsequent running away from home and finally our capture. All the kids were talking about it and I felt quite famous. At the end of the day Richie and me proudly walked towards the school gates, side by side, with our arms cross- linked behind our backs in the chariot fashion. Suddenly, before we had even exited the school gates, I saw stars. Mum had been waiting behind the dustbin area to ensure that I had paid attention to her strict instructions not to associate with Richie. She must have taken quite a swing at me, because coupled with the element of complete surprise it really was a 'clump' to remember; and it really hurt. For the very first time I literally saw stars. Although dad 'spared the rod' mum certainly didn't!

Mum could be quite a 'fiery' person. It would not take much to get her to go out and fight for our cause. Many are the times that one of the older boys would give me an unsolicited, and unwarranted 'clump'. Regardless of the reputation of the family concerned, mum would slip on her 'Bat-cloak' and go and do battle for us, just to ensure the bullying didn't happen again. Our family life was very settled and calm. It was an extremely enjoyable family environment that I would dearly like to relive, without changing a single thing. To the best of my knowledge there was only one really furious row and I can recall it vividly. For the first 22 months of my life I did not even see my dad because he was part of British Forces in Europe fighting the Germans from early 1944 until November 1946, when he was 'demobbed' and then returned to Silvertown. The three of us were in the middle living room and I remember looking up and seeing mum screaming furiously at dad, "I'm leaving you!" Although I was under two years of age I remember this incident with absolute clarity. I was completely terrified and I crawled across the floor gathering all my favourite toys together, as they were strewn across the room at the time, and through my tears I cried out "I'm going with mum." I vividly recall all my confusion at this event, being very worried that I could not seem squeeze all the toys into the small cardboard toy box.

I discovered in later adult life the cause of the furious row was mum had discovered that dad had been 'playing away'. It was while he was serving in H. M. Forces in Germany. Apparently he was billeted with a German family on a farm and had a very good relationship with the farmer's daughter. The result of that relationship was a baby girl. Dad had been talking to John and Florrie Roder, who lived next door at number 9 Westwood Road, and had left his jacket on the wall outside their house. Later, when they found the jacket still on the wall, they looked in the pockets for identification and found a letter to dad from a German girl called Eva. The letter said that her father was very annoyed at what had transpired, but would forgive dad and give him a good welcome if he returned to live with Eva and his daughter in Germany. The Roder's thought mum should be made aware of the letter. I was told that mum ran in to Nan's house, next door but one, and told her that it was all over and she was leaving dad. I do believe that the thought of mum and me moving in with Nan must have absolutely terrified her. Apparently, she got quite annoyed and told mum to 'pull herself together' because all this happened at a time of War and that soldiers didn't know whether they would still be alive or dead on a day-to-day basis. She said that things like this happened in War and that mum must accept it. I am glad to say that common sense prevailed and eventually life returned to normal at 11 Westwood Road. Although if there were any small 'tiffs' between mum and dad that escalated to a row mum would then shout out "Why don't you go back to Germany?" but this did stop after a year or two.

In summer 1956, at the age of eleven, I finally left West Silvertown Primary School. I was delighted that I had been accepted at South West Ham Technical School, in Canning Town, right opposite the bombed out Trinity Church. Things had also changed around our local parade of shops. Gladys Hobbs had left the grocers shop at the corner of Eastwood Road and John and Amy Pattison were the new owners. I believe this was also around the time that Ray Griffiths gave up his grocery shop on the corner of Barnwood Road. It was around this time that I became aware of Robert T., who stood outside Tate and Lyle, Plaistow Wharf all day, every day, as protest about being given the 'sack', apparently for insubordination. Bob was an electrician and also the Union Shop Steward. Apparently, he was called to the Chief Engineers office to discuss a problem and there was a difference of opinion between Bob and the Chief Engineer. It was claimed that

Bob subsequently became very verbally abusive to the Chief Engineer, who promptly sacked him. Bob then started his many years of sole-picketing and he always stood at the very bottom of the Canning Town / Silvertown viaduct right opposite Lyle's factory by the telephone kiosk and the street newspaper vendor Carlo's newspaper stand close to the 669 bus stop. Soon after the picketing began the Chief Engineer said that he would re-instate Bob if Bob apologised, but Bob wanted the Chief Engineer to apologise to him!

Bob was a great guy who would pass the time of day speaking to anybody who approached him. An intelligent, striking, elegant man; tall, slim, tanned, grey hair swept back, well spoken, with piercing blue eyes if I recall right and always seemed to be wearing a light coloured mackintosh. He was clearly a man of principles and I do admire his single-minded determination, because regardless of the weather conditions he would be there, day after day and year after year. He was never taken back and I dread to think what effect that must have had on his family life. Bob's brother was head of security at Lyles and the story goes that he had to instruct all of his Commissionaires not to let Bob enter the premises, so that must have also had an added family complication. After the many years of picketing it must have really got to Bob, because I remember that he used to carry a small notebook and would suddenly look over to either lorries or staff coming and going into the factory and scribble down notes.

In 1967 Lyles factory ceased to become a production refinery, relying on just syrup packaging and distribution, so the high level of management was no longer needed at Plaistow Wharf and senior production managers were transferred to Thames Refinery in East Silvertown. Bob followed them and for a period continued picketing outside Thames Refinery. Alternative employment was so very easy to obtain in those days as you could walk from factory to factory along the huge industrial route from Silvertown Services Lighterage Ltd at Clyde Wharf in West Silvertown right up to Henley Cables in North Woolwich choosing where you wanted to work. Bob became very well known in the area and not just by locals but also people passing on the busses as 'The man who stands outside Tate & Lyle.' If I were in that situation, then I think I would just have looked for another job.

10

Secondary Education

On my first day at South West Ham Technical School in September 1956 I sat on the number 669 trolley bus with Jimmy Laing, from Evelyn Road, who also attended SWHT. He was two years older than I was. I felt quite proud in my new grey school blazer and cap. There were a few wisecracks on the bus from some of my school friends who had not passed the 11 plus examination and were on their way to Pretoria Secondary Modern School in Canning Town. Nothing malicious, because we were all good friend's, but just good-natured 'what a prick I looked' in my new school uniform. As we got off the bus in Barking Road, at the bus stop just outside of W. E. Norris & Son pram shop, I followed Jimmy across the road into the Brewsters newsagents shop on the opposite corner, next to Chas. Hyman tailor shop. Jimmy bought either the Hotspur or Rover comic and I followed suit. I wasn't sure whether or not I would like this new 'boy's own' comic because I was used to the more frivolous and childish fully illustrated comics. I need not have worried, because pretty soon I became hooked on these new comics. That addiction continued for about two years at which time I then became hooked on more occult reading material, like Fate and Prediction magazines and at the same time 'flying saucer' books, like

South West Ham Technical School – rear view of playground area

George Adamski's 'Flying Saucers Have Landed' and general books on the occult and reincarnation.

I settled down at South West Ham Tech. and the first couple of years were fairly uneventful. I found the studying difficult and I thought the homework was quite a time consuming imposition. It interfered with me going out and playing with all my friends who attended Pretoria School, as they did not receive any homework. I enjoyed English, but found the Mathematics and Algebra almost incomprehensible. I enjoyed reading books and was a frequent visitor to the Public Library situated above Tate's Institute in Wythes Road, Silvertown. Given my age the male librarian was surprised at my interest in reading material consisting mainly occult, flying saucers, space travel and mysticism. He was absolutely bowled over when I ordered H. P. Blavatsky's 'The Secret Doctrine' and when the huge book arrived I can recall him saying, "I just don't know how you will get on with this one, but it's certainly beyond me." Suddenly, I had seen a new book cover pinned on the 'new books' stand. It was nothing like my current reading matter. I was strangely drawn to the photo on the front dust cover of this new book and asked if he could show me the 'Manual of Karate' book by E. J. Harrison. I had completely mispronounced the word 'Karate', but he kindly put me right with his pronunciation; which I now know was also incorrect. For some unknown reason the book absolutely fascinated me and it was almost a weird foresight of things to come. Little did I know that ten years hence karate would virtually take over my life and that I would also become a black belt instructor, running a karate club, in a sport that would occupy me for the next 25 years.

There were small changes to my life from around 1957. For a start, for the very first time I was allowed to wear long trousers. These were standard 18-inch bottoms, light grey SWHT School trousers purchased from Leaches, the school outfitters in Canning Town's Barking Road. Also, I had suddenly taken much more of an interest in the girls and in order to 'dress the part' I started taking on so many 'part time helper' jobs that the pressure of it all made me feel quite ill. Also in 1957 dad finally decided that our radio days were over and decided to buy a television. I'm glad in a way that he left it that late because had he made that decision a year earlier I would have probably missed out on the 1956 final third series of the renowned radio series of Journey into Space. We went to the Globe Radio & Television shop at 116 Barking Road, Canning Town, to purchase the TV set. Dad decided to buy the Bush 14inch screen Mahogany case TV. Funny how almost all Television sets were charged in guinea's in those days and the price of 59 guinea's comes to mind for the cost of this particular television set. Fortunately for me the renowned Murkoff's ice cream shop was right next door to Globe Radio & TV shop and coincidently right in front of the bus stop, so dad, on a high after his new acquisition, treated me to a large Murkoffs vanilla ice cream cornet before we got onto the 669 bus and carried the TV back home.

We set up the TV in the corner of the front living room and then after moving the arms of the 'V' shaped indoor TV aerial and sticking it in as many area's as the six feet of aerial cable would allow, and altering the line hold and frame hold TV controls, we finally found a spot in which we received a reasonable picture. Now granddad, long retired from his Jubilee pub potmans job, had trouble walking without using his walking sticks and he had also become quite deaf. He only lived next door but one and apart from listening to the radio his only other pastime was using a pencil to shade in parts of photographs that appeared in the Daily Mirror newspaper, or drawing individual bricks on a plain sheet of paper until he had built a wall. So television was quite a new experience to granddad and I'm quite sure that he thought it was bordering on magic. After we had the TV for a week or so, granddad decided to make the difficult journey from his house to our house to have a look. Mum encouraged this trip, quite proud of the fact that we had bought this modern device and was keen to show it off. In all honesty it was the only new thing I can recall dad ever buying at that particular time, because most things we bought were either second hand or just given to us. It was a very difficult trip for granddad to make because of his extreme difficulty in just putting one foot in front of the other, even when using his walking stick, so he couldn't just pop in and out again – once he was in he was in for the evening!

We had no indoor baths or showers in those days so granddads hygiene was not of a very high standard. He could not and did not bath. Once he arrived in our front room lounge he plotted himself up on a chair so that he could rest his left elbow on the sideboard and cup his left hand around his ear to catch and intensify the sound waves from the TV. If he had moved any closer to the TV then he would have obscured our view. Because he was quite deaf, granddad always shouted. On the very first night of viewing he turned his head towards us and shouted out, 'Is the sound on, I can't hear it?' Dad turned the set up in slow degree's each time saying, 'Can you hear it now Jim?' By the time granddad, hand still cupped to left ear, said, 'Just about' it was truly deafeningly loud to us! Also irritating was that granddad would, in a loud voice, talk back to the telly. I'm sure he thought that many of the fictitious programmes were for real! The other problem was that he stunk the room out! As there were no baths in our houses in those days and granddad was far too big for the old tin baths that hung on the outside yard fences, his personal hygiene left a lot to be desired. You sort of got used to the smell after you had sat in the room for a bit, but for a newcomer entering the room it was like inhaling from a bottle of smelling salts; and you could see a recoil action in their eyes from the impact of the stench. Looking back, I was particularly unkind one smelly evening, because for a joke I dug out our only surviving WW2 gas mask, with the luminous green bottom canister attached. Then, wearing it I walked into the lounge and sat on the floor in the middle of the room to watch the TV. Mum went bananas! Dad bit his lips to suppress a smile as mum aimed a clout at me. 'Get out!' she shouted. As I jumped up to run out of the room I heard granddad shout out, 'What's he arsing about at?'

Naturally, all this overly loud TV sound and the pong spoilt all of our prime viewing time and we all blamed mum for this; after all she was the one keen to get him into our house. Prior to the TV purchase I cannot recall my granddad ever being in our house – now it was every night! It would have been unkind to have stopped his nightly visits, because the TV had opened a new world to our virtually housebound granddad, but clearly we could not endure this situation long term – the Airwick jar with the absorbent fabric plunger pulled out to maximum was constantly operational in the front room. We were all quite desperate – this could not continue. Both long retired and quite elderly nan and granddad could not afford to purchase a TV set, so after mum and dad had a meeting and discussion with the rest of the family a family whip round resulted in sufficient cash to purchase a TV set for them. Granddad was delighted and things in our house returned to normal.

11

Swimming like a fish

I enjoyed my sport too much to really get into my studies in the manner that the prestigious SWHT School required me to. I represented the school in boxing and swimming. It's strange that I ended up quite a good swimmer, because my initial introduction to swimming was very traumatic. I was nine years of age, back in my Primary School days in 1954, when I first heard about the forthcoming swimming lessons.

Back in the 1950's West Silvertown parents did not live in fear of persistent crime, or paedophiles abducting their children, therefore we were free to come and go as we pleased – even as nine year olds! I did not have to keep on reporting my current whereabouts to mum, so I thought nothing of pre-empting my first swimming lesson in 1954 by going it alone. Given that my very first Primary School lesson was one month away, I thought by then, with a bit of practice, I would be able to swim. I made enquiries and discovered that the swimming baths were miles away. They were in Balaam Street, at the Abbey Arms. Now I knew Balaam Street, because this was one of the areas that mum had previously visited for Social Services. I knew there was an office just past the swimming baths and I am sure that this was one of the 'pick-up points' when I had previously been placed into the children's convalescent homes.

Looking back I cannot believe I did it. It was a tremendous journey to make for a nine-year-old in those days. Mum of course had to agree to my swimming plan; otherwise I would never have the money for bus fares and swimming pool fee. Mum thought it was an excellent idea, but as my first official swimming lesson was still one month away I did not have a costume. "Never mind," said mum "We'll find one of dads." Well, dad was never a regular swimmer and I doubt that he would have bought a swimming costume since his single days. Mum pulled out the only available swimming costume from the copper, in the corner of the scullery. The copper had never been used in my short living memory. Had I not seen my Nan toiling away with her copper, vigorously stirring the bubbling content of clothing with the long copper stick, and all but disappearing in the cloud of steam, I would never have known what our copper was used for. On washing day Nan's scullery was like a modern day sauna, what with the heat from the fire under the copper roaring away and the water above bubbling like mad. The boiling clothes, washing powder and added soda crystals had a distinctive stench all of their own. Fascinating stuff and I can still recall the smell today.

I can also still smell the musty stench of dad's old swimming costume, as it must have laid in there for years. Had the attendant opened my towel I am sure I would never have been allowed in the pool. Anyway, when mum opened the costume it was the old type Victorian gent's one piece – just like the ones women wear, with the two straps over the top. Also, it was a sort of woollen material, maroon coloured and marginally short of being home knitted! Although we didn't have a full view mirror the expression on mums face told the story – it was hideous! I was still desperate for the early swimming lesson and, as necessity is the mother of invention, I had a brainwave. What if I didn't use it as a full one-piece costume, but folded the top shoulder straps down and kept turning until the costume was the same size as my pants. I could then use my elastic snake belt to keep the whole thing together. We tried it and it sort of worked. My legs were so skinny, which made the whole thing look more like a maroon pair of baggy shorts than a swimming costume. Nevertheless, it would suit its purpose and finally get me to the swimming pool.

After catching two buses to the Abbey Arms, I arrived at Balaam Street swimming baths and asked the lady for a ticket. The woman asked which pool I wanted, large or small? I said that I didn't know and she asked if I could swim. I told her that I couldn't swim and that this was my very first visit, as I had never been in a swimming pool before today. She said, that in that case I would be best off in the small pool and to be careful. From memory the entrance fee was just four pence. The small pool was tiled white throughout and was much larger that I had expected it to be. I got into one of the cubicles and changed into dad's swimming costume. What with all the folds it did bulge quite a bit either side of the elasticised snake belt around my waist. I walked out of the cubicle and for a short time watched people both jumping and diving into the pool. I walked around the pool a couple of times, looking for a spot that was not too crowded. I found a nice little spot, in what I now know was bordering the six-foot depth of the pool. I thought, here we go and I just jumped in like the others.

I hit the water and began thrashing my arms and legs about, in a quite uncoordinated fashion, but nothing was happening. I was under the surface and swallowing water. I kept on thrashing about and I was now aware that I couldn't breath. Every time I opened my mouth I took in more water. I was also acutely aware that I could not hear anything other than completely strange muffled sounds and for a moment a panic came over me and I thrashed about in a frenzied manner. The discomfort and panic seemed to go on for a long time. There was no pain, but I suddenly lapsed into unconsciousness. The next thing I recall is lying by the side of the pool with the attendant kneeling over me doing his resuscitation. I was coughing and spluttering and a bit panicky, as what with the water coming out of my mouth I found it difficult to breathe in air. Then all of a sudden I was all right again. The attendant asked me why I had jumped in the deep end if I couldn't swim. I told him that I didn't know that it was the deep end and he just shook his head in disbelief. Although I was now terrified of the water he insisted that it would be best to go back into the shallow end of the pool with someone who could swim. I suppose this was just to get my confidence back. There was a very sympathetic woman with him, possibly also an attendant, and she led me down the ladder in the shallow end and I had a brief walk about with her. She was very helpful, getting me to grip the bar at the side of the pool and raise my legs to the surface, doing a paddling motion with my feet to keep me horizontal. My confidence was restored. On returning home I never told mum what happened and I never visited the swimming pool again, prior to having my first official school lesson a month later. I received my quarter mile proficiency-swimming certificate signed by the West Ham Mayor, Daisy Parsons, in early 1955.

12

Hair of the Dog

The years 1958 to 1959 were also quite memorable. At the age of thirteen I became eligible to be a 'paper boy' and asked Jean Docherty, owner of the newsagents shop, if she had a newspaper delivery round available. Fortunately, I was in the right place at the right time and she gave me a paper round delivering newspapers to six streets, including Westwood Road, and also The Ram public house for twelve shillings and six pence per week. Delivering newspapers to The Ram was always a pain, because it was such a long journey down the North Woolwich Road, right past Lyles and Pinchin Johnson factories and immediately after Clyde Wharf. Also, they had a large German shepherd guard dog that would wait by the letterbox and grab the papers with a growl as I endeavoured to squeeze them through the tight letterbox. The first time it happened it made me jump, as the dog hit the door with a bang and a growl as he grabbed the papers. Once I was over the initial shock and I got used to it, I would torment the dog by just pushing the papers in the door a bit and then pulling them out again, before he had time to grab them. The dog always knew the time I would call, so he was always waiting for the daily 'contest' we had. This went on for months and some times I would torment the dog by growling back at him. I wish I hadn't done that because one Saturday, for some reason or the other, it wasn't convenient for me to deliver the paper at my normal 7.00am time. I delivered the paper around 10.00am and as I approached the door I could see that it was open and that someone was cleaning the step. As I arrived at the doorway I came face to face with the large German shepherd dog.

I looked at him and he looked at me, clutching the bundle of newspapers. I thought "Oh no!" and I imagine the dog thought 'Gotcha!' As our eyes met I saw him tense and a sort of change came over his face. Instinctively, I knew he was going into 'attack mode' so I stupidly threw the newspapers through the doorway and turned and ran for it. I had probably gone about 15 metres, turning sharp left by the railway crossing into North Woolwich Road when he got me. I was wearing a light green jumper that my Aunt Alice had knitted for me and he caught me in his jaws just below my left shoulder. The force of the impact knocked me to the ground between the railway lines and the dog started to pull at my cardigan. It seemed to be entwined in his teeth. He looked big before I was lying down, looking eye to eye with him now he looked enormous! Suddenly, whoever was cleaning the step had got hold of the dog by its collar and was shouting and pulling it off. I jumped up and feel sure that I must have beaten Roger Bannister's 1954 four-minute mile record as I shot by Pinchin Johnson's and Tate and Lyle factories to our parade of shops.

On arriving home I promptly related the incident to mum, who was furious and said that I should immediately return to The Ram to 'sort it out' with the owner. I told mum that there was no way I was going to return to The Ram with that big Alsatian dog around. Mum put on her black 'Bat coat' and said "Come on my boy, I'll take you." At that point I thought there was a danger of the owner of The Ram telling mum about the every day tormenting I had inflicted on the dog for months. I told mum not to worry, because I would go back later on my own when the pub opened at mid-day and the dog would, hopefully, be locked up. If mum had discovered that I had regularly tormented the dog it would be worse for me. I sheepishly returned to the pub, just after mid-day. I had sort of pulled at the damaged area of the jumper, just to make it look a bit worse than it was originally.

The lady owner was very apologetic about the incident. She said that if the cleaner hadn't witnessed the attack she would never have believed it, because it was so out of keeping of the dog's usual good nature. Great, she was unaware of all the long term early morning teasing that I had inflicted on the dog. Upon examining the jumper she did say that she was surprised at the damage the dog had done, so perhaps I did overdo the enhancement a bit. She said that if I gave it to her she had some one who could professionally repair it for me. At that point I thought that it wasn't worth coming back just for that small recompense. She then told me to wait by the door and disappeared back into the pub. She returned with a ten-shilling note in her hand and said that she wanted me to take this partly as a belated Christmas present and partly to compensate me for the trauma of the dog attack. She said that I was the best paperboy that they had ever had because I delivered so early that they were still in bed and the dog alerted them to the fact that the papers had been delivered. They said that prior to me they never got their newspapers until mid-day.

I was over the moon! Ten shillings, I just couldn't believe it, because ten-shillings was a lot of money in those days. How could I keep it from mum? Mum would want her cut that's for sure. I used to have to give mum two shillings and sixpence from the twelve shillings and sixpence I got for doing the paper round. Mum said that it was a contribution 'towards my keep'. So, I bought sixpence worth of paradise fruits, which were soft centred boiled sweets, just to get some change. I went home to mum explaining that the jumper would be repaired and that I had got four shillings and sixpence left from the five shillings the publican gave me. Mum said that she thought that was quite generous and then took two shillings and sixpence of it as a bit extra 'towards my keep'. I was happy because I had still got seven shillings left!

13

Factory raid and a near death experience.

It was around this time that the large British Road Services depot in Bradfield Road closed down. Like true professional scavengers, a gang of us were in there the following day. Clambering over the large, securely locked, double entry gates we ran amok throughout the three-story office complex. Having mock fights from room to room and throwing twinlock files and other abandoned bits of office stationary at each other. We had a whale of a time and discovered that if you climbed through the skylights in the toilets on the top level you were actually on part of the roof. Looking over the parapet it was a long way down.

By comparison to the offices we found the factory area quite boring. We had a bit of a laugh jumping into the lorry inspection pits, which were quite deep, but that was about as far as excitement went in the factory, until we discovered the locked box-cupboard attached firmly to the wall. We were making such a racket, which because the whole complex had been evacuated echoed everywhere, that I am quite surprised that no one passing outside called the police. It took quite some time, and a lot more noise, to finally break open the locked cupboard doors. Given that they had been locked we thought that there must be something quite exciting, or valuable, inside. What an anticlimax when we just saw row upon row of tins. When we opened the first tin there was just a white powder inside. Reminded me a bit of the National dried milk. When we tipped out the powder onto the floor there was also a large circular glass container with a colourless liquid inside.

I think somewhere we must have found reference to fire extinguishers, because we suddenly realised that these were all refills for fire extinguishers. We scooped the powder into a heap, stood back, and one of us threw the large glass container of colourless liquid onto the white powder. From memory, there was limited, and certainly disappointing, foam produced. To enhance the effect we then had the bright idea of breaking open all the tins of powder into one of the deep inspection pits. We could then all stand at the side of the pit and throw the glass containers simultaneously. This took quite some time to achieve and it was agreed that one of us would enter the inspection pit and with a piece of cardboard scoop all the powder into one large heap. Richie, the friend I ran away from home with, agreed to jump in and do what was necessary. We all had a bit of a whisper and decided that it would be a great laugh if we threw our glass containers into the pit before Richie had time to get out. Of course, we had no idea at the time that the content of the glass containers was acid.

Simultaneously, we threw our glass containers into the pit. Richie jumped out of the way and there was a hissing and foaming. Suddenly Richie started holding his face and shouting that it was burning and hurting him. I am sure that we could see some pockmarks appearing in his flesh as the acid started reacting with his skin. We hurried him out of the building and rushed him round to Mrs Green, the nurse who lived in Barnwood Road. I recall that she treated his burns and I believe he may have been left with some minor scarring. All in all we had a great day in the British Road Services depot. Clearly we had found a new camp here and I eagerly awaited our next adventure the following day.

There we were the next day having a great time in our new camp, making just as much of a commotion as we had previously when someone shouted out "Coppers!" I looked around and saw about five policemen entering the factory area through the large doors. I ran like mad into the office area racing through the corridors and up the stairs until I came to the toilets. I hid in one of the toilet cubicles hoping I was safely hidden, but I could hear adult voices, getting closer.

I was a great climber and looking up from the toilet cubicle I could see one of the half open glass sky light windows. I placed my foot on the toilet seat and hoisted myself up to the skylight and through the small gap onto the roof. I laid low and kept quiet. I waited just by the skylight to see if the policemen would search the toilets. Peering through the side of the skylight I saw them enter the toilet and jumped back quickly. Did they see me? I was unsure, but had to make a very quick decision because although the flat part of the roof by the skylights was about 150 yards long and five yards wide, there was no escape. If they had seen me and squeezed through the skylight I would have been caught. My mind was racing, trying to think of a way out. Then I remembered the very long drainpipe that I had seen running down the side of the building every time I had passed by the BRS depot. Given that I was quite an ace at negotiating drainpipes, given my prior experience up and down West Silvertown Primary School roof, I had often looked at this drainpipe with a sense of awe. To me it was the 'Mount Everest' of drainpipes and I had quite often fantasised about trying to shin up to the top and get down again. Little had I known at that time that one day I would have no choice but endeavour to negotiate a passage down that drain pipe.

I'm sure that anyone who had climbed up the side of a steep cliff, or very long drainpipe, and found it scary will confirm that it's a lot scarier coming down. This crossed my mind as I ran over to the parapet and looked over the top. It was a very, very long way down and to make matters worse, looking to the right I saw two of the old style 'Black Maria' police cars parked about fifty yards down the road, just by the double entry gates. Looking left I saw the drainpipe, but it did not go right to the top of the parapet. The parapet was about a metre high and there was a small gully where the roof joined the parapet to allow rainwater to pass through the parapet into the drainpipe on the street side of the building. I realised that there were probably no police in the cars, as they were all chasing us. Therefore this was my best escape route.

Stan Dyson

I ran to where the gully was and looked over the top. It could not have been better! At the point where the water runs from the roof through the gully and into the drainpipe there was a huge metal funnel area that would be ideal to stand on. I hoisted myself onto the parapet and looked down again. I felt a bit queasy. It was a very long way down and some inner voice kept whispering 'don't do it'. I felt that I had no choice and swung myself round and dropped over so that I was on the other side of the parapet, with my feet on the funnel top of the drainpipe, looking towards the skylights. I had an empty feeling and a fluttering in my stomach as I took my left hand off the parapet, at the same time bending my knees and with my left hand feeling downwards for the funnel top of the drainpipe. To reach it I had to slide my right hand towards me, away from the roof side of the parapet to the very edge. I finally felt the curved edge of the top of the drain pipe and then very slowly rested my left knee onto the thin edge of the metal funnel at the top of the drainpipe and that was it; I was completely stuck, unable to move in any direction, with my right hand clinging onto the top edge of the parapet for dear life and my left hand gripping the top of the funnel alongside my bent left leg that was pointed outwards, away from the building.

I'm not sure what was hurting me more, the rather sharp thin edge of the funnel top digging into my bent-up knee or my fingers clinging onto the rough concrete of the parapet. I just knew that I was going to die. I remember thinking that I hoped it wouldn't hurt too much and I was feeling dizzy just thinking about the fall. Then I remembered the fall that I had survived with just a broken wrist from Lyle Park house. I squeezed as tight as I could to the wall and turned my head to the right, looking for the park house. There it was about 100 yards away and the first floor windows were far below me. So, no, I would not survive a fall onto the pavement below. I was too old to start crying now and just thought what a waste it was and how I wished the police had caught me. Suddenly I heard voices shouting up. "Don't move sonny, whatever you do don't move." It was the police, so they hadn't seen me. I could have stayed safe on the roof after all. "We are coming to get you down, don't move at all."

One of them shouted up "Can you hang on until we get the fire brigade?" As much as I had previously enjoyed my 'fire-lighting' days and subsequent rides on the fire engines there is no way I could have clung onto the parapet that long. My raised right arm was beginning to cramp and my fingers, clinging to the edge of the parapet were numb. West Silvertown Fire Station was just about half mile away between Fort Street and Mill Road, but it had briefly crossed my mind what if the firemen did rescue me and shouted "Not you again!" One of the policemen shouted, "How did you get up there?" I replied "In the toilets, through the skylights." I cried out "I can't hang on much longer." A policeman replied loudly "If you fall you will die son, so hang on tight!" The fact that a policeman had told me I would die took away any foolish notion I had that I may somehow just break bones again and gave me an inner strength to bear the pain. After all, considering the alternative I felt I now had no choice but to hang on for dear life.

Suddenly I heard footsteps running across the roof and looking up I was face to face with two very annoyed looking policemen. Strong hands grabbed my right arm. "Let go and give me your other hand," said one of the policemen. "I can't" I said, "I'm frightened." The policeman replied, "It's the only way we'll get you up, sonny", as he leant over the parapet and grabbed the top of my jumper. With one of them pulling my right arm and the other my jumper I was finally hoisted over the top of the parapet to safety.

The two policemen were naturally non-too pleased. One of them said "What do you think you were doing, sonny?" as he cuffed me around the back of the head. He continued, "Do you realise you put us all in danger?" Two further open handed smacks from the other policeman whacked across my ear. As we arrived at the skylights I could see what he meant because as a skinny thirteen-year-old it was considerably easier for me to squeeze through the narrow opening of the skylight and drop down into the toilet cubicle than it was for the police. As we exited the factory by the small side door, which was surprisingly open now, I noticed that now there was only one police car in attendance. Unfortunately, the local community policeman complete with his bicycle had now turned up.

This was most embarrassing for me as it was only a few weeks ago that he had caught me standing under one of the streetlights at the bottom of Knights Road throwing stones up trying to break the bulb.

At that time he just administered his summary justice by giving me a couple of clips around my ear and taking me home to mum. And it was only last week that he caught me with mum's large Sunday roast carving knife as we were using it for target practice, throwing it into one of the fences in Lyle Park. Mum had no idea that I had sneaked it out of the house. This policeman was nearly always in Lyle Park. He would sit in the park keeper's hut chatting to Mr Creagan and Mr Rickets, the two park-keepers, so I really should have known better as the fence was right next to the hut. He didn't clump me this time, as I was not doing wilful damage of any kind. He took the large carving knife from me and asked me "Where did you get this toy from?" I told him that I had taken it out of our house and he asked if my mother knew that it was missing. I told him that she didn't and he said "Well, we better walk home and tell her then." The very first words he said to mum as she opened the door were "Is this the type of toy you let your boy play with?" Needless to say that gave me more practice dodging about under the table and gave mum the opportunity to sharpen up on her broom poking skills. Getting back to the roof rescue saga, the very first thing the community policeman said on seeing me was "Not you again!" which made me really glad that they had not called out the fire brigade. I would have been really embarrassed to hear them both shouting "Not you again!" in unison.

The two policemen from the car took my name and address and asked me who else was involved. So, I had been the only one caught. I later found out that the others had not rushed upstairs like me, but straight along the office corridor and out through the side door that the police had either broken open, or somehow unlocked. I said that I did not know them as they came from the other part of Silvertown. Obviously, they did not believe me, but the community policeman chatted with them for some time and I believe he convinced them that he could best deal with this small incident on his 'patch'. He started to walk me home to mum, again. I begged him to let me off this one, as mum would have gone berserk. He stopped and talked to me for some time about the danger I had put myself in. He also asked when would I grow up and get some sense. Did I realise that I could quite easily have died? He asked which school I went to and when I told him South West Ham Technical School he could not believe it. By now he was calling me 'Stan' and explained that his experience of me during the last few weeks led him to believe that I was on a downward spiral. I told him that I wasn't really bad, just adventurous and a bit boisterous.

He said that if I gave him an absolute promise that I would not commit any further criminal acts, like breaking into locked up factories again, or irresponsible acts like taking and throwing about large knives he may not find it necessary to escort me home for some more of the usual summary justice that mum dished out. You bet I agreed! His trust in me meant that we became friends and from then on, especially when in Lyle Park, I was on best behaviour and acted more responsibly.

Stan Dyson

Aerial view of Silvertown & Royal Docks 1940's

Silvertown Life

Aerial view of West Silvertown & Docks 1950

Stan Dyson

Trolley buses and Silvertown/Canning Town Viaduct 1952

Silvertown Life

West Silvertown parade of shops 1962

Stan Dyson

Barnwood Road 1960

Silvertown Life

Boxley Street 1950's

Stan Dyson

Westwood Road 1950's

Silvertown Life

John, Kathleen, Stan & Roger Dyson

14

Brace yourself boy, this is really going to hurt!

Also, around this time, as well as my newspaper delivery round I started another part time job helping Wag Bennetts paraffin delivery van to deliver paraffin to both West Silvertown and the Silvertown Station areas. This was quite a hectic job, because first I would board the 669 bus from the bus stop just opposite the West Silvertown Doctors surgery and get off at the bus stop opposite the Rose of Denmark pub at the bottom of the viaduct at Canning Town. I would walk the short distance to Wag Bennetts cycle and motorcycle shop and help fill up the large cylinder that was attached at the rear of the van, with paraffin. We would then drive back to West Silvertown and I would knock at all the doors from Cranbrook Road to Mill Road asking if anyone wanted to buy paraffin. We would then drive to Silvertown Station and I would again knock on all the houses from Andrew Street to Lord Street selling the paraffin. Although I only got five shillings for this job, I didn't get any pocket money from dad and when you are just thirteen every penny counts.

School life ticked on and I did find the going rather hard. It was at the age of thirteen that I received my first disciplinary 'thrashing' from

Mr Baxter, the SWHT Headmaster. We were trying to liven things up in the chemistry lesson and had just incurred the teacher's wrath by flooding his desk. In the Chemistry room the teacher's desk was very long, with a small sink in one corner with a long thin tap, shaped like a curved cane at the very top. The taps had a long rubber tube attached that ended in the sink, so you would be unaware if the tap was actually running. We stuck the plug in the plughole and turned the tap on to a very slow trickle. It was a double lesson, lasting all morning and the teacher was sitting marking books and we watched as the water reached the top of the sink and, with the surface tension, then bowed slightly above sink top level. Suddenly the water completely broke the surface of the sink and edged towards the teacher. It collected around the pile of books he was marking and then around his elbow. He was furious when he finally noticed it, but we all played dumb and suggested that the tap must have been left slightly on for ages and that it was certainly nothing to do with us.

That took us up to the break period and we had a good laugh in the playground about his damp elbow and the wet homework books. What could we do to liven up the second period? Someone suggested writing the swearword 'Fuck' on a piece of paper and then slipping it into one of the unmarked homework books. We all drew straws and I got the short one. I said that I was not going to write 'Fuck', but as we had all sworn to 'do the deed' if we had drawn the short straw I said that I would write the word 'sexual intercourse' on the paper. The others complained that I was trying to 'weasel out' of the agreement, but finally saw things my way. I crept back into the classroom early and slipped the piece of paper into the books that the teacher was marking. When the teacher discovered the inch high letters scrawled across the piece of paper he hit the roof. We all had to stop work and he demanded to know who had written "this foul word" as he put it. We stuck to the agreement and no one owned up. He then said that unless the culprit admitted it there would be no lunch break and that we would all be back kept in after school hours for detention, which would last until the person responsible came forward. That was it for me, so I stood up and said, "I did it." He looked at me and said, "I'm surprised at you Dyson" and held the offending article out for me to collect. I thought that considering the circumstances he had taken it quite well, but there and again I liked the chemistry lesson and I always had good marks from him, in fact I was one of his favourites, or so I thought.

Smiling, with the rest of the class jeering and laughing, I took the piece of paper with the offending words off him and smiling turned to walk back to my desk. "Where are you going Dyson?" he said. I turned and just looked at him. "Take it down and give it to Mr Baxter" he said. I recall screwing my face up and saying "Oh, Sir?" He pointed to the door and shouted, "Get out!" I walked down the corridor and knocked on Mr Baxter's door. "Come in," he shouted. I walked in and told him that the chemistry teacher had asked me to deliver this piece of paper. He told me to put it on the desk and dropped his head down and continued writing. I waited for a moment, then he briefly looked up again and said "You can go now, boy." Clearly he was very busy and as tempting as it was to leave, I just knew that I must stay. I said, "I think he wants you to read it now, Sir." He picked it up and looked at it for a long time, and then he looked at me and said, "Did you write this boy?" I replied, "Yes Sir." He said, "Why?" I explained that it was just a joke. He asked if I knew what the word meant and I thought it best to play dumb and said, "No Sir, I don't." He replied, "In that case why did you write it?" I shook my head from side to side and hunched my shoulders, hoping to look as pitiful as possible.

He asked where I first heard the word and I said it was in the playground. He asked me who first uttered the word in the playground and I said that I didn't know the person. He shook his head and said, "I don't believe a word you are saying." He asked what sort of a home did I come from to which I replied a good one. He asked if I had any brothers or sisters and I replied that there were four of us. He asked if I was the eldest and I confirmed that I was. Waving the paper he then said, "That's a good example to set to the others then, isn't it?" I then said, "No, it isn't Sir, and I am very sorry." He seemed to mellow a bit and started lecturing me on how the eldest must set an example to the siblings as they look to the eldest as a role model. It was at this stage that I was beginning to feel a bit more relaxed and nodded in approval at everything he said. I was beginning to feel sort of 'let off the hook' when suddenly his secretary, Miss Cohen, knocked on the adjoining door and said "Excuse me Mr Baxter, can I have the cane and the cane book, please?" He replied, "Not just yet, I'm going to use it!"

He looked at me and said, "Yes, I'm going to cane you Dyson. I view this incident so seriously, that I am considering writing to your parents." I thought 'No, not Batwoman' and coming after the pulling down girls' knickers at the dock fence saga, this would be the icing on the cake for mum. She really would rant on for ages over this one. He asked if I would rather him write to my parents or increase the thrashing. I didn't hesitate to reply that I would prefer the increase of the 'stick'. I thought that he may respect me for that, but in any case it's good for your playground kudos afterwards. He took the cane out of the other desk in the corner of his room. "Right boy, turn around and face the door, bend down and touch your toes," he said. I replied "Can I have it on the hands, Sir?" as I knew that you can ride the blow a bit on your hands, also you've got two hands to share the load – you've only got one bum! "Certainly not boy" he replied, "I want you to be able to write afterwards." As I bent down I tried going halfway, just so my bottom wasn't so tight. He wasn't having any of it and made me do bending exercises until I became more flexible and could touch my toes with ease without actually bending my knees. He said, "Move one inch and we won't count that one." Just before the first stroke came whistling down I looked at his office door and thought briefly that if someone came in at that very moment the door handle would hit me right in the head.

There was a millisecond delay in me hearing the swish of the cane coming down and it connecting with my very tight bottom. I suppose it's a bit like being shot, you see the flash, feel the pain, and then hear the bang. On impact, I flinched and my fingers came off my toes to just above my ankles. I hoped that he didn't count that as a 'movement' and start from square one again. The pain wasn't as bad as I thought it would have been. It hurt, that's for sure, but not as much as I had anticipated. There was about a ten to fifteen second delay, whilst he composed himself and gave my bottom a couple of gentle taps with the cane as he lined me up for the next strike. Then there was another swish of the cane and another reflex flinch by me on impact. By now the impact area of the first strike was really beginning to hurt, as the initial numbness had now given way to a burning pain. Then there was a third swish and impact. At this point I let out a loud 'Ouch!' and stood up, rubbing my hand over my bottom and looking back at him. "Who told you to get up then, boy?" he shouted. I said "Sorry, Sir" and got back down. As the fourth stroke hit me it was agony and the thought did cross my mind that he may have been a descendent of Captain Bligh. I stayed down, gritting my teeth, waiting for the next one. He said, "That's it boy, unless you want more." I replied "No Sir." He finished by saying "Off you go then and any more incidents like this and it will be six strokes and your parents." On leaving his office I thought, thank God I didn't write 'Fuck' on the paper.

As I walked back to the chemistry class my bottom was on fire, it really did hurt. When I entered the classroom the chemistry teacher asked what happened. I told him I was caned. "How many strokes?" He asked. I told him it was four. "Where?" he asked. I thought 'blimey', how macabre can you get and replied "On the backside." He sort of winced and said "I'm sorry I sent you down there Dyson." Of course, that made me feel a whole lot better. I wriggled about on my seat for ages. At lunchtime we all went into the toilets and I dropped my trousers so the lads could have a good look. All backside canings had to be verified, to stop people boasting they had taken double the number of strokes. My four stripes came through with flying colours, in fact two of them had blood specs on, so I was held in great esteem for the rest of the day.

It was around the age of thirteen that I first started boxing and swimming for the school for the school. I think that dad was a bit disappointed that I hadn't followed up the family tradition of football. My Granddad was a very good footballer and both my dad and his brother Jim had followed in my Grandfathers footsteps. Jimmy Dyson was Captain of Middlesex Wanderers and prior to that played for Enfield Town F.C. Dad had devoted his football life to playing for Tate & Lyle first eleven football team. I think his greatest achievement was in 1952, when Tate & Lyle first eleven won the Barking League. The trophics dad won for that triumph occupied the mantelpiece in our front room for years.

I must have been about eight years of age and recall my deep disappointment on discovering that my main Christmas present was a size five leather football, pair of football boots and football shorts and top. I remember that dad took me over to Lyle Park on either Christmas Day or Boxing Day and made me kick the football about with him. He was shouting out instructions and giving me tips on ball control and seemed to be having the time of his life. I hated every moment of it! It was bitterly cold and had actually started to snow. I couldn't wait to get home and play with the present my Nan had bought me which was a silver coloured plastic ray gun. It was like a rifle and as you pulled the trigger it emitted a sound and a white card with red stripes moved backwards and forwards in a crude attempt to simulate fire. I loved it and it gave me weeks of fun. After the disappointing football gear presents and disastrous and freezing football practice in Lyle Park I distanced myself from the sport for the rest of my early life.

The age of thirteen was also the time when I was allowed to spend solitary holidays at my Aunt Alice's house at Purley, in Surrey. I really enjoyed the Purley holidays and fell in love with Maureen Taylor, the girl who lived next door but one to my Aunts house at 77 Northwood Avenue. Maureen was a tall, slim, well-spoken, beautiful brown-eyed brunette with an almost constantly smiling face. She was my very first real girlfriend. We were really like chalk and cheese, as I was the rough and ready cockney East London boy and she was the posh country girl. We really did get on well though and had great times together. I always looked forward to school holidays just to stay with my wonderful Aunt Alice and see Maureen again. I have very fond memories of this period.

I first met Maureen the prior year when I was twelve when Mum and Dad used to take us all to Purley in summer 1957. Maureen and me really hit it off right away. We just sort of bumped into each other as we simultaneously walked down the steep flight of steps that led from our respective houses into Northwood Avenue. We just acknowledged each other, and then we started chatting and didn't stop. It's as if we had always known each other. When I returned home to Silvertown I used to write to her and also 'phone her up from the telephone kiosks beside both Victoria Dock entrances at the bottom of the Canning Town / Silvertown Viaduct and also the entrance at the bottom of Mill Road. Mill Road Victoria Dock entrance telephone kiosk was the most convenient because from the age of 13 I also used to sell the evening papers to the workers as they 'knocked off' from both the Docks and the Flour Mills, every thirty seconds or so I would loudly shout out 'Star, News and Standard, Star, News and Standard'. 'Old Man Carlo', as we used to call him, had died and his son had now taken over his father's evening newspaper round and he asked me to help him out by covering Victoria Dock gate. I believe that some of the workers used to just take the newspaper and forget to pay, so I was there really just to hand over the paper and collect the cash. He also had newspaper stands at the other Victoria Dock entrance at the bottom of the Viaduct, outside Lyle's factory and at the bottom of Knights Road.

The relationship that Maureen and I shared ended through circumstances out of our control in 1959, but it still endured over the years albeit that we never saw each other. I would often wonder what happened to her, and then under really bizarre circumstances we regained contact by telephone in 1989. Initially I told her that I was 'an old boyfriend.' Maureen replied, 'John?' My heart sank, and I thought she'd forgotten me. I said, 'No, it's not John – it might have been before John; I may have been your very first boyfriend.' Maureen immediately replied, 'Stanley Dyson, is that Stanley Dyson?' 'Yes', I replied, 'it's me.' Maureen told me that she didn't recognise my voice, but that she had wondered what become of me over the years. Well, it had been quite a long time and I had by now lost my cockney accent. We exchanged a couple of letters explaining what had happened to us over the years and then arrangements were made for Maureen to come over from where she lived in Luton with her husband to visit us in 1990. I was very excited on the evening of the visit, but also nervous. We were kids when we last met and there was a real danger that as adults we would have nothing in common, after all, 32 years had passed since we last saw each other. I need not have worried because the moment I opened our street door it was as if the thirty odd years were just a weekend. The relationship was just the same, but we were just bigger kids. Also, the childish inhibitions had gone; whereas all those years ago I had fantasised about kissing her, but too shy to attempt it, as soon as I opened the front door and greeted her we kissed. Maureen and her husband Ian plotted up with us in our lounge and Maureen and me just babbled on. Suddenly, after about half hour we stopped talking and realise we had our respective spouses sitting there, just watching us. We never let the relationship lapse again and I still see Maureen today.

15

The price you pay for fashion

At last I reached fourteen! At this age I took serious interest in girls and fashion. On the fashion front I really needed to get my act together. The only clothes mum and dad ever bought me were school uniform replacements. They had just replaced my baggy 18-inch bottom school trousers with a new pair of 16-inch bottoms and what a job it was convincing dad that 16-inch bottoms were not Teddy boy type drainpipe trousers. He seemed to think that they were just about borderline "looks a bit on the tight side" he said. Well, all the rage at the time was the new 14-inch bottom drainpipe jeans. I now had the old 18-inch school baggie's, which were now surplus to requirements, at my disposal to bring me bang up to date. I recall sneaking them into Nan's house and asking to borrow her sewing kit. I told her that I was going to convert them into 'modern' trousers and swore her to secrecy. Nan laughed as she got out her sewing kit and I knew that she would not breathe a word.

Off came the turn-ups and I slit the seams all the way up the inside to the crutch. I thought that it would be best to leave the outer seam, being, the most visible, untouched and that later proved to be a big mistake. Nan did not wish to become involved in the deception and therefore she took no part in the alterations. Over a period of two nights I altered the trousers to just under 14-inch bottoms. I took my time with the stitching and the seam around the bottom of the trousers wasn't too bad. That's more than I can say about the inside leg seam. What I did not count on was that taking trousers in by the inside seam leaves a huge bulged area around the crutch that by comparison makes male ballet dancers crutches pale into insignificance. It looked like an outsize cricket box had been jammed down my front. What a codpiece! Fortunately, I had a sort of drape jacket that had been given to me by the man who lived in the house next to Gallerfings Café in Westwood Road. Provided I ensured that I had a safety pin firmly fixed, anchoring the jacket about two inches below the bottom button, there was no problem because the huge crutch bulge was covered. The only problem was if I had to take my jacket off, but then, the girls really loved it – they thought it looked just great!

As we approached summer of 1959 I realised that I would have to discontinue wearing the jacket that covered the huge bulge in the crutch of my trousers. I was now at the age of extreme girl interest and clothes were of major importance. I urgently required some modern gear to promote my image and it was no good looking in dad's direction. I still had the paper round and Saturday paraffin delivery job, but that was not enough. I urgently needed to find more work to feed my proposed clothes habit. I started to ask around. My first work enquiry was purely by accident.

One Friday I lost my school free bus pass and having no money, I started to walk home. As I was walking through Rathbone Street, towards the Canning Town viaduct, I passed Alexandra's shoe repair and bag shop. Poor old Mrs Alexandra seemed to be struggling dealing with a number of customers. I stopped and asked her if she needed any help. She asked if I could stay with her and cover 'watching' the stall and also pack all the bags away and take the mobile stall to the storage area around the corner. Yes, I said I could stay and thereby got another small job. It was a busy job, selling the bags, then clearing the stall of bags and storing them in the back of the shop afterwards. Then finally wheeling the trolley just around the corner to the storage bay.

No money had been mentioned and the thought did cross my mind as to whether she may have thought I had just volunteered to help as an act of goodwill. When I returned to the shop, after storing the market stall, Mrs Alexandra was about to lock up the shop. She thanked me and said I had been a great help, worked really hard and saved her a lot of bother. She then handed me a ten-shilling note. I couldn't believe it, ten-shillings for just an hour and half's work. That was a lot of money and I was delighted when she said "Can you make it at the same time next Friday?" You bet I could! On Fridays in school I ensured that I was on my very best behaviour and my punctuality was spot on, because I could not afford to end up on a needless detention because that would cost me money now. Thereafter, on Fridays I used to run from school to Mrs Alexandra's shop just to ensure that she got the maximum value for her ten-shilling wages. She was great and she always had a nice hot cup of tea and doughnut ready for me as I arrived.

On the off chance I also called into Pattisons Grocery shop, on the corner of Eastwood Road, early on Saturday morning and asked if they needed any Saturday help. John Pattison said, "Can you start now?" I told him that I could and then immediately started my next job. This meant cancelling my Wag Bennett's paraffin delivery job, but John Pattison was going to pay me Thirty shillings for helping Monday to Thursday evening, after school and Saturday morning. John's mother, Kate Pattison, ran the green grocery shop next door and asked if I could help her out Saturday afternoon for five shillings. The very first job I had to do when I arrived in Mrs Pattisons shop was to put my fire lighting skills to good practice and get her fire underway in the living room. She was very appreciative and complimentary about skills in this area saying, 'No one lights a fire like you do Stanley.' I was now in the money, but not as much as I should have been because mum put up the house keeping money to twelve shillings and six pence per week. So I was doing Jean Docherty's newspaper delivery round just to pay mum off each week.

I enjoyed working in John Pattisons grocery shop, especially Saturday mornings because I used to deliver peoples grocery orders and would generally get a tip between three pence and six pence. I always kept the tips a secret, just in case mum found out. There was one round I particularly enjoyed delivering to a couple at the end of Knights Road. He was an Anglo-Indian and his wife was a very attractive redhead. We all sort of hit it off from the very start. They were very good to me and always used to invite me in for a cup of tea and a chat.

Stan Dyson

John Pattison had an adult male assistant who, when I returned to the shop, quite unkindly used to say, "Why does it take you so long to deliver to the Indian Princess?" She was a very attractive lady and I think he was jealous. I got on so well with the couple that I used to return to their house of an evening and assist them with their decorating. Mrs Pattison was a funny person to work for at times. She had a 'thing' about carrots. As Mrs Pattison was huddled over the fire in her living room I ended up serving in the shop. Although I never handled the money I used to 'weigh-up' the green grocery orders. Mrs P., as I used to call her, had a large bag of carrots in her living room. Whenever anyone wanted carrots I used to say "Just a minute" and walk into the living room and ask if I could serve some carrots. Mrs P. used to say, "Who are they for?" She would then get up and look through the curtains into the shop and if she liked them she would allow me to serve. If she did not like them then I had to walk back into the shop and say "Sorry, no carrots left." Unfortunately, there were an awful lot of people she was not too keen on, because I turned away more than I served. Subsequently she had a large sack of carrots just rotting away. This used to drive her son John Pattison from next door absolutely mad. He told me to take no notice of her and sell them anyway. Who was I to argue with the person paying me?

I was now getting up at 6.00am for the paper round and then helping with both the grocery and green grocery shops Monday to Thursday after school and all day Saturday, then Mrs Alexandra's shoe repair shop Friday after school. Then, in between all this, I was trying to fit in my extensive homework every night. I was beginning to feel a bit run down and tired. I clearly recall thinking that I hope it isn't as hard as this when I finally start work. Then to cap it all Hyme Secunda, who sold ladies and gents wear in Rathbone Street asked me to work for him Saturday afternoon. He offered me more than Mrs P., so I told Mrs P that I had so much homework, working towards my GCE's, that I could no longer work Saturday afternoon for her. So, I ended up with about five shillings less from Pattisons and agreed to share my time between the grocery and green grocery store. Overall I ended up five shillings better off with what Hyme Secunda paid me. I was always on edge when working in Secunda's because Mrs Alexandra's shoe repairs was just about five stools further down Rathbone Street and I had previously told Mrs Alexandra that I couldn't work Saturdays because of my homework. Talk about life gets complicated; I had a lot of dodging about to do!

My life was so hectic, I felt as if I was on a fast merry-go-round and I was too afraid to jump off. I wanted to give up some of the hours I was working, but you can only get money by hard work. I knew that it could only go on for just under two years, and then I would be starting work so I decided I just had to soldier on. Back in 1950's Silvertown 'tally-men' were very popular. That was a sort of hire purchase that came direct to your door. There were no contracts or signed agreements, you just ordered what you wanted and the following week it was brought to your door. If you liked it then you kept and were given a payment card. Each week the tallyman would call and you would pay what you could afford, generally two shillings and six pence or five shillings, until such time as you had paid for the goods. The two tallymen servicing West Silvertown were Mr Elford and Mr Herbert. I ended up buying my clothes off of Mr Herbert, who would call each week accompanied by his daughter to collect payment. They were very pleasant people and I would never have dreamed of 'knocking' them. Given the poor conditions that we lived in I would not be surprised if they did get caught from time to time. I only purchased small items of clothing from them because I was saving like mad to purchase my very first new suit from Granditers Tailors in Canning Town.

16

The trouble with snogging is…

I started visiting the Silvertown Station and North Woolwich Park area's in 1959 and 1960. It seemed much easier to strike up relationships with girls outside of your immediate area. We used to hang about around Drew Road School and North Woolwich Park. Generally I would be in the company of Terry Farmer, Alan Brown, Mickey Taylor and Billy Marler, but one of the best early 'girl scouting' evenings I spent was with Willy Travers and two of the North Woolwich girls at the beach area, near the playground in North Woolwich Park. It was dark and we were sitting on the rocky slope beside the Thames. Some very serious 'snogging' went on for what seemed like hours. I was quite dizzy with it all and finally, for the very first time, I plucked up enough courage to slip my hand under the girl's blouse and fondle her breasts. I was beside myself with delight. It felt soft, warm and very nice, but I wasn't quite sure why I liked it so much, but I decided that's as far as I had the courage, or the right, to go in my first serious smooching session. In the end I felt quite exhausted with it all and the girl was breathless. I actually had to help her up and support her a bit as we walked away. She looked sort of exhausted and half-asleep. I'm not sure whether I was so good that I wore her out, or so boring that she was nodding off. I remember that she said she was concerned that she had stayed out longer than she should have and that her mum would be 'doing the rounds' looking for her. I didn't know who her mother was, but I was soon to find out.

Suddenly, mum was bearing down on us walking up the road at the side of Woolwich Gardens towards the sloping beach area. She seemed to know her daughter's haunts. I was so surprised when I saw her mum, because I knew her and she knew me! She was quite a well-known local figure who was the Warden in the swings and paddling pool area and had actually exchanged strong words with me earlier that day. She looked none too pleased in seeing me supporting her daughter. I had absolutely no idea that was the girl's mother, because fortunately the girl looked nothing like her mum. Mum's raucous outcry was an immediate antidote to the girls' somnambulistic gait. She said, "Oh shit!" and hurried off towards mum. That was the only fondling I ever had with that girl, but it was to be superseded by another, far more memorable one, in the not too distant future.

We were not always chasing the girl's, we had other enjoyable games. One of my favourites was two onto one stone fight's. Generally it was Peter Pocklington and Terry Farmer onto me. After ensuring we had an ample storage of stones in our pockets the action would start at Mill Road with me walking backward towards Silvertown Station. All the time I would be throwing stones at them, they in turn would pick them up and throw them back at me. This would go on all the way up the bridge stairs at Silvertown Station and into Factory Road right up to the North Woolwich Pier. Then I would walk along the riverbed, throwing stones at them as they walked along the slanted river wall at North Woolwich Park, until we reached the beach area, my 'snogging' spot. In all the weeks we played this rather dangerous game none of us were injured by the missiles, until I threw one at the rocky gradient that Terry and Peter were standing on. I hadn't even tried to hit one of them, but the stone ricochet off of the rocks and hit Peter in the temple. He fell down the rock and I thought that he had knocked himself out. Fortunately he wasn't seriously hurt, but that was enough for us to realise what a stupid game it was. We never indulged again.

The Adventurers Youth Club at the top of Drew Road School was like a magnet to us West Silvertown lads. Neil Sedaka had just released his 1959 single 'Oh Carol' and I just could not get enough of it. Fortunately for me they played it all the time at the Adventurers. I hadn't been there very long when I was 'banned' by the Warden. A couple of the lads gave me a wind-up about a nice looking girl who they said fancied a 'long snog' with me in the Principals office, right at the very top of the stairs. I kept on pushing them for a name and my mind was running riot trying to guess which one of the girls it could be. I even started to smile at some of them, just to see if they showed out a bit. In the end, with my hormones running wild, I agreed to take potluck. They had told me that once this girl has kissed you know you've been kissed and how lucky I was that she fancied me. They said that at a certain time the Warden pops out and is generally gone for about half-hour. They said that the office lights go out and that the girl would be waiting in the small toilet at the back of the office. I was so excited and full of anticipation. I was wondering how far we could go in half-hour. Being a veteran now of 'boob squeezing' I had mentally decided to get this part of the fondling out of the way as quickly as possible, which would leave about 20 minutes before the warden came back.

I stood in Drew Road playground and looked up at the Wardens office. Suddenly the lights went out and I waited until he had walked out of the school gates. My knees were shaking in anticipation. They said "She's up there and waiting for you" and to cries of "Lucky Bastard" I started the long steep climb up Drew Road school stairs. I was trying not to run, as I did not want to arrive breathless. As I arrived at the Wardens door I wondered whether it would be locked and all this was a wind-up. I had never been up this last flight of stairs before, so I was a bit nervous. I opened the door and sort of crept over the threshold into the darkened room. I had no idea where the toilet would be and sheepishly said, "Is there anybody there?" There was no reply and I thought then that it was definitely a joke. Then again, sounding remarkably like a medium at a séance, I called out a bit louder "Is there anybody there?" This time, from the left-hand corner of the room a soft female voice replied, "Yes, is that you Stan?" I sort of whispered back, heart pumping and nervous beyond belief "Yes, shall I come in." She replied "Of course."

My mouth was dry and my heart was pumping. I cannot begin to tell you what courage it took for this fourteen-year old to feel his way across the darkened room towards the toilet door, full of anticipation as to which girl it would be and what would happen. There were at least half dozen I would have liked it to have been and wished I had checked the dancing area beforehand, just to see who was missing. Suddenly I was in the toilet. The window was wide open and I saw the silhouette of a girl. She dwarfed me, she was huge, and confused I stopped in my tracks. The toilet was small and our bodies were touching. She immediately got hold of me and squeezed me into her. I could feel quite large boobs pressing against my chest and her lips were pressed against mine, her mouth was open and seemed to almost cover my face. I could taste her lipstick. To be honest, it felt quite pleasant and with the right girl it would have been absolute heaven. She spun me round so that my head was almost out of the window. My back was arched and my head was being pushed right out of the window by her aggressive kissing. I was trying to prize her lips off mine just to see her face. I heard a lot of jeering from far below in the playground, so yes; this was definitely a set up.

Suddenly, I was successful in pulling my face away from her and I saw who it was. She must have been about two or three years older than me and she was huge. Not in my mind at all attractive, to be honest quite repulsive, and I fought my way past her, running across the office just as the lights went on and straight into the arms of the Warden. As I ran by him he actually swung a clump at me shouting, "You're banned!" Cheeky fat bastard, if it had not have been for the embarrassment of being caught with that certain girl I would have run back and challenged him to try and clump me again.

Apparently, as soon as the Warden had got about 100 yards down the road a couple of the lads who had set me up ran after him shouting out a warning that someone was up to no good in his office. We all had a good laugh about it afterwards. My face and lips were covered in bright red lipstick and the trick they played on me ran to military precision. I told them all to watch their backs because I would certainly get even with them, in my time.

17

Something for the weekend Sir?

Sex, sex, sex, that's all we seemed to talk about at school, especially during the Metalwork lessons. Quite often in Metalwork I was paired with a boy called John Jolley. What with all the noise in the Metalwork Shop the teachers could not hear all our idle sex chat. If only they had GCE 'A' levels in Sexology – we would have passed with flying colours. We almost continually fantasised as to what it would actually be like having sex with a girl for the very first time, as opposed to the ritual daily self-abuse we all seemed to indulge in – despite the alleged threat to our eyesight and the rumour that the persistent daily abuse could send you completely mad. Well, the only fear we ever had was that the very first time you had sex with a girl you could end up making her pregnant. There was one boy who worked part time in a Newsagent shop and he used to steal packets of cigarettes and sell them off cheap. We asked if he could also lift some condoms for us, but unfortunately the Newsagent did not stock them so it was up to us to obtain them ourselves. So, I decided to purchase a packet myself, just in case the anticipated splendid event came up suddenly; fat chance of that really though, but I thought I'd be prepared. I scouted all the local chemist shops along the Barking Road from Rathbone Street right up to the Abbey Arms, but they all had female staff and there was no way I was going to ask a young girl for a packet of contraceptives. I decided that the best bet was a Barber Shop and the ideal place was in the very small parade of shops just before Woodstock Street, which was the second street along the Barking Road from Rathbone Street, that had a tailors shop called Pollocks situated on the corner.

At the start of the small parade of shops there was a Turkish man who owned the Barbershop. I sort of cased the joint a bit trying to pluck up enough courage just to enter the shop, and I always looked through the door to see if the Barber was alone. Unfortunately, most times he was cutting someone's hair and as I appeared, staring through the glass-fronted doorway, he always looked up and we were then eyeball to eyeball. As a cover I always used to buy a packet of spearmint from the 'Beechnut' spearmint machine attached to the wall immediately outside. With every 4th purchase it used to give out two packets – I ended up with so many packets that I could have traded wholesale in spearmint. I was so nervous about asking for the first time, and what should I ask for - a packet of Durex, condoms, a packet of three, or perhaps just 'something for the weekend Sir?' What if he asked why I wanted them? I was actually wearing part of my school uniform, so what if he questioned me about my age? I wasn't old enough to smoke yet, let alone indulge in full sex with a girl. Anyway, one day he was alone, and as I stood outside, looking in, our eyes met and I nervously opened the door and walked in. He was a swarthy man wearing a white Barbers overall and typically Turkish he had a thick black moustache. 'Yes?' he said, looking me straight in the eyes. Running around my head was 'Er, can I have a short back and sides please'…but it actually came out as a squeaky voiced, 'Can I have a packet of three please?' What an anticlimax! He didn't even bat an eyelid! He just opened the glass doors pulled a packet out and took my 2/6d. With heart pounding I made a hurried retreat, just in case he changed his mind. Outside I cradled the precious packet in cupped hand, constantly reading it, 'Durex Gossamer Lubricated' wow, just wait until I get back to school and show the lads. This was easily worth the 2½-days dinner money it had just cost me.

Back in school this was really good for my kudos, even just flashing them around drew a lot of attention to me. Some of the kids offered me double the price for them. The jealous one's questioned why I had bought them. 'You 'aint even got a girl friend yet, 'ave you Dyson?' 'Wot they for then Dyson, an expensive trial run wank?' 'You can't make a cardboard bog roll tube pregnant, so wotja buy 'em for Dyson?' Most of the jealous comments were from the boys in the next year up. After the initial novelty had worn off and the tension of hiding them each night at home, poked right up my bedroom chimney every night, because mum was always going through my pockets, I thought that I must really put them to their intended use – before they exceed their 'use by' date!

Having now at last broken the ice with the Turkish Barber shop owner I returned a few times over the ensuing weeks and purchased more packets of condoms. This was not just to keep my hand in, but also to supply other SWHT mates with 'packets of three' as we called them – and I made one-shilling profit on each sale! Finally, the great moment arrived for me with the opportunity to finally put the well-hidden and treasured condoms to good use. Three of us were confined to the second floor school laboratory classroom as a lunchtime detention. We carefully filled the condoms to capacity with water from the laboratory taps, and then after tying a knot in the tops we water bombed the kids in the playground below. I must admit that although I regretted the improper demise of the condoms I was relieved at the prospect of no longer continually transferring these items from pocket to pocket in different jackets and the daily task of both poking them up and retrieving them from my sooty bedroom chimney stopped.

18

Paying the price of 'bunking-off!

With all my jobs and now my new hobby of girl hunting, I was pretty well wasting my time at school. Also, at the time I was knocking around with Alan Brown who used to live in Westwood Road, but had recently moved to Custom House area. Alan also attended South West Ham Tech. and regularly played truant. I followed suit, taking the odd couple of days here and there. I would get my mum to write a note stating, "My son, Stanley, could not attend P.E. (or football, swimming etc.) at school this week" or "Stanley could not attend school swimming on Monday and Tuesday because" followed by the reason. I would then take tracings of the note and use it to create a new letter omitting 'P.E. at', or 'swimming at', making the letter read "Stanley could not attend school on Monday and Tuesday because etc." The school therefore never questioned the letters, as they looked identical to mums.

We started our usual 'long weekend' by having just Monday and Tuesday off school and this dragged on to Friday. We had never played truant for a full week before. On Monday I started off to school at my usual time, only to be met by Alan at the school gate. He said that he did not have his letter prepared, so can I just have this last day off with him and we would both definitely return to school on Tuesday. Despite hearing warning bells ringing in my head I foolishly agreed.

Next morning I had a sort of premonition and as I heard the post come through the letterbox I ran to pick it up. There was a letter with the West Ham Education logo on it addressed to dad. I discarded the other mail and started to walk upstairs. Mum was too quick for me! "What's that you've got, my boy?" she said as I passed her on the stairs. I said that it was a letter for me, which was a bit daft because no one other than Maureen Taylor, from Purley, ever wrote to me. She said, "Show me." So I quickly flashed the letter. Mum was insistent that I give her a proper look at it. She then said, "That's not for you, it's for dad."

As I waited upstairs on the landing I could hear her holding a conversation with herself, saying that it looked an important letter and should she perhaps open it. Clutching at straws I was hoping that it was not connected with my truancy. Suddenly mums voice boomed up the stairs "What's your plans for today then, my boy?" "You didn't go to school last week, did you?" she said. I asked to see the letter, but she wouldn't show it to me. I tried to lie my way out of it by saying that Miss Cohen, the school secretary, must have accidentally got the wrong name. Mum wasn't having any of it. Out came the bat cape again and mum transformed into Bat-woman about to embark on another urgent mission.

I went to school ahead of mum and was sitting in my first lesson for about half hour when I was summoned to Mr Munden, the new Headmaster's, office. Batwoman was sitting there looking smug. Mum loved dealing with people in authority, putting on her voice. It was all "Yes, Mr Munden, No, Mr Munden." Mr Munden asked me who I was with last week. I said, "I would rather not say, Sir." He said, "I already know and want you to now confirm it was Alan Brown, wasn't it." I confirmed that he was correct. They then held a conversation about me, as if I wasn't there. Mum was saying that on the whole I was a good boy from a good home and she thinks that I had been led astray. Which is pretty much as any mother would say. She must have felt pity for me, standing there to attention, with the entire colour drained from my face. That is until Mr Munden made his next comment about my general high absenteeism. Mum said "What?" "He always attends school, he's rarely sick."

Mr Munden then got up and opened the adjoining door and asked Miss Cohen to bring in Dyson's absentee file. That's it I thought, I'm

The Jubilee Public House 1960

completely rumbled now. Batwoman was giving me the evil eye as Mr Munden opened the file containing all my forged letters. Mum looked at the letters and kept saying, "Yes, that's my writing but I didn't do that one, or that one, or that one." Mum looked at me and shouted, "Who wrote all these letters?" I simply replied "Me." Mum stood up and I think she felt so embarrassed that she was about to clock me one around the back of the head. Mr Munden must also have anticipated mums course of action because he got up and said, "I think that I ought to deal with this now Mrs Dyson because it becomes part of the school disciplinary procedures." He continued, "Thanks for coming Mrs Dyson and rest assured that I will ensure that Stanley is fairly and suitably punished for this. Mum thanked him and left. Mr Munden sat at his desk for some moments looking at all the forgeries, comparing them to one or two of mum's original letters. He looked up and said sternly "Well, we have a master forger here, haven't we Dyson?" I just said "Yes, Sir." He said, "Out of curiosity, how did you do it?" I told him and he said, "I thought so."

He asked me what I thought I was doing at the moment. I said "Just wasting my time Sir." He stuck his face into mine and hissed,

"You're right!" He then sat down and asked me about all the prior truancies. He also asked what I had done in the prior weeklong truancy. I answered honestly, no point in lying once your caught. He asked me what I did in my spare time and I told him about all the part time jobs. He was amazed and asked me to run through it all again. He sat there and shook his head. I just wanted to get it over with. I felt that all this protracted questioning was torturous, when all I wanted to do was turn around, bend over, stare at the door handle again and wait for the flogging. I was sure that it would be six strokes for this one and given the pain that the four strokes had given me I was not looking forward to it.

He got out the cane and the cane book and placed them on the table. I can assure you that standing there looking at the instrument of torture magnifies the pain well before the application. Knowing what a disciplinarian Mr Munden was, I started to wonder if he would be bringing the cane down harder that Mr Baxter had previously. My backside was beginning to hurt even before I had actually bent over! He stared at me for quite some time and I remained firmly at attention. He sat back in his chair and said, "You know Dyson, I don't think at heart you are as bad as you portray yourself." I replied "No, Sir." He said, "Don't keep on saying just yes and no sir." "Tell me what you propose doing about it." Holding up some papers he said, "Look at these last reports, they are a disgrace." "What are you going to do about it boy, because you haven't got much time left?" I replied, "I will change now, Sir." He said, "Good, we're getting somewhere." "Would you like to strike a deal to knuckle down to it, instead of a thrashing Dyson?" My heart leapt, and he no doubt saw the relief on my face. I replied, with the start of some involuntary tears welling in my eye's "Yes Sir, I would like to get down to some serious studies and I won't let you down." "Well, Dyson" he said, "Do I have your absolute word on that?" I looked him straight in the eye and said, "Yes, Sir you do."

He continued by saying "I'm going to put you on report, boy, for a period of three months and I want to see a visible improvement, do you understand?" I replied "Yes, Sir." He then said, "What will you say to your friends when they ask how many strokes of the cane you got?" I replied, "I will tell them whatever you want me to tell them, Sir." He replied, "I suggest that you tell them to mind their own business

Dyson, now get out there and get your act together." I will never forget the faith he had in me and, as far as school was concerned I was a changed person. I did not let him down and my greatest achievement was in a subject I hated, that was Metalwork. In that year I turned it around from the normal bottom of class to top of the class.

I understand that Alan Brown was not as repentant as I had been. From memory, he did get a thrashing and it wasn't too long after that event that he left SWHT prematurely, to start work. I believe that the fact that mum had actually attended the school did me a lot of good, because mum was very supportive of us all and had obviously painted a fairly good picture of me and our home life to Mr Munden before I arrived in his office. When I got home that evening mum asked what happened and I told her that I had decided to knuckle down to it. She asked if I was caned and I said, "Yes, I got six across the backside." Mum winced and said, "I bet that hurt." And then she said, "I hope you learn from that, my boy, and turn over a new page now." Good old mum, she never told dad.

19

Shoot up's and first entrance to the saloon

As far as leisure time went, apart from chasing after the girls from the other end of Silvertown and North Woolwich, I used to play with George Beautyman who lived at 19 Westwood Road. George had the upstairs part of the house and lived with his mother, Daisy, and younger brother, Terry. The downstairs part of the house was originally occupied by Daisy's sister, Violet, and currently by June and Peter Curran and their daughter Susan. I am ashamed now, as an adult, that one of our 'games' was to torment Freddie Turner whose back yard was facing George's back yard. Poor Freddie was mentally impaired in some way, what my mum used to term as 'backward'. I have no idea of his age at the time, but would estimate he would have been in his early forties. He was tall, thin but in a very muscular sort of way and always had a shock of curly and untidy light brown hair. Freddie was immensely strong and always very cheerful. He used to help out in Mrs Pattisons green grocery shop before I did. He would do the entire heavy lifting and tipping out of sacks of potatoes and other labour intensive work required in the shop. Although, according to Mrs P he was absolutely useless at lighting her fire. He appeared to love peanuts as he was continually eating them and always seemed to be wearing a light brown cotton fabric work coat, like the type someone in an engineering workshop would wear.

Well, George and me would look out of the upstairs back window and see Freddie sitting in his backyard. We would then get our bicycle pumps and a bowl of water and then siphon the water into the pumps. We would then go downstairs into the yard and creep up to the fence, which fortunately for us was quite high, and standing on two milk crates we would point the 'loaded' bicycle pumps over the fence and discharge the water. We would then leap down and run upstairs to watch Freddie's puzzled expression as he peered over the fence. When he settled down we would repeat the 'torment' again. The third time we were quite overt about it. We actually leant over the fence and doused Freddie with the water. On running upstairs and looking out of the window you could see that Freddie was furious. He was almost climbing over the fence and would look up at us, face contorted with rage, shouting incomprehensible words at us. With the look on his face I dread to think what would have happened had those immensely strong hands actually got hold of us.

During the 1959 school holidays I took George over to my Aunt Alice's in Purley for the week. We had a great week there and God only knows how my aunt tolerated us all week. As I was a lot taller than George was I went into the local sports shop to buy two 'GAT' .177 slug guns. I would have preferred the 'Diana' air pistol as it was slightly more powerful, but they cost more. When they asked my age I said sixteen, as I was unsure of the legal age for buying a slug gun, and walked out of the store with the two weapons. We were an absolute menace all week. We shot up most of the apples on next doors tree, which led the man to complain to my aunt. I vividly recall poor Aunt Alice coming all the way up the different levels of her garden to tell us off, as we were sitting on the top level at the time. As it was such a walk I suppose she thought she would carry her washing up and kill two birds with one stone.

I was lying on the top-level lawn while Aunt Alice lectured us about the dangers of using air pistols indiscriminately and said how annoyed her next door neighbour was at having his apples polluted by lead pellets. With 'GAT' pistols they were more a pneumatic than an

Stan Dyson

air pistol as after firing you would need to depress the spring loaded barrel back into the gun before unscrewing the pin at the other end and loading a lead pellet. Well, as Aunt Alice had her back to us, hanging washing on the line, I picked up a small hard twig off the lawn and found that it just fitted into the pistol barrel. Without taking aim, and with no intention of hitting my Aunt, I fired in her direction. Now GAT slug guns were notoriously inaccurate, God only knows how we managed to even hit some of the apples on next doors tree, but this time the missile found it's mark. It hit Aunt Alice in the fleshy bit above the elbow and stuck in. She immediately dropped that particular piece of washing, let out a howl, turned and said "Stanley, how could you." I was so upset myself seeing my Aunt crying with blood running down her arm, and thoroughly ashamed because I had not meant that to happen.

In order to continue with the holiday we had to hand the two guns to our Aunt for safekeeping. That probably saved one of us our sight, because having got bored with shooting at targets we had got to the stage when we were discharging the weapons at each other, using the trees as protection. My girlfriend, Maureen, had now moved further down the road to Kenley and I told George that I would take him round and introduce him to her. Unfortunately, as we crossed the bridge near Kenley Railway Station we bumped into Maureen's mum. As mentioned previously, Maureen's mum was none too keen on this East London 'tearaway' and she made it quite clear that she did not want me knocking at her door for Maureen. So, that was the end of my association with Maureen and I am quite sure that Mrs Taylor, my Aunt Alice, her next door neighbour and the rest of Purley were pleased to see the back of us at the end of that week.

At fourteen years of age I could go into the Jubilee pub and buy alcohol, or so I was told by Granddad, who by now was having great difficulty in just getting about on his walking sticks. Granddad should know, because he had previously been the 'pot-man' there for many years. Between the ages of eight and eleven many is the time I would walk the 50 yards down Westwood Road to the Jubilee, then climb up on one of the stools that stood outside and shin up onto the window ledge. Then, looking through the window, I would peer around the inside of the pub until I saw granddad collecting all the empty glasses, and then just bang on the window to attract his attention. He would look up and seeing me would then wave the back of his hand towards me and shout out, "Bugger off!" He knew full well what I wanted. "Can I have thrupence for an ice-cream Granddad?" Thrupence was the old type three-penny piece. Again, granddad would shout out "Bugger off." And again I would shout back "Can I have thrupence for an ice-cream please granddad?" Eventually, he would then make his way to the saloon bar doors, stick his hand out with a three-penny piece and shout, "Don't come back!"

Granddad gave me his glass tankard and asked me to go into the saloon bar and ask for a pint of mild and bitter. He preferred draught beer to the bottled beer, which he thought was too gassy. The very first time I tried it I was very nervous, because as far as I was concerned only the men went into pubs. As I entered I felt as if every adult eye was on me. Then Harry Bowden, the owner came over to me and just said "Yes?" I handed over the tankard and asked for a pint of mild and bitter. Harry said "Whose that for then?" I replied "Granddad." He smiled, took the tankard and starting to pull the pint said, "How is the old sod then?" Great, I had passed the test!

Granddad really appreciated that because it meant that he now had a regular 'go for' for his favourite tipple. At last all those years of giving me three-penny pieces were paying off. We were all still having trouble with mum's brother, Danny. When he was 'off the drink' he was a likeable rogue. I remember that when I was about nine mum gave me a one pound note to run an errand. Passing the Jubilee on the way to the shops I saw Danny sitting on the stool outside. "Hello Uncle Dan." I said. "Hello Stanley." he replied, "Where are you going?" I told him I was running an errand for mum and at the same time I held up the one-pound note. "Tell you what", he said, "Give it to me and I'll give you ten bob and tell mum you lost it." Naturally, I refused and it did immediately dawn on me that I could, if that way inclined, had said that I had lost it anyway and kept the pound. When I told mum what her brother had said she was furious and took me to him for a sort out. Danny didn't care and he just laughed it off saying that I had got a vivid imagination.

20

Punch-up's galore!

I did feel sorry for Danny once though. He had become such a pest that most of the residents of Westwood Road, who were 'regulars' in the Jubilee, way-laid Danny one night and tried to 'run him out of town'. He was sitting on the wall just outside our house. About a dozen men and women surrounded him and he was trying to defend himself. They were shouting that they were fed up with his bad behaviour and he should 'get out' while the going is good. I stood at my front door watching. Individually they would have been terrified of him, but there is courage in numbers. There was a lot of jostling and I even saw one of the smaller, really timid men, give him a good hard push. I think that before ambushing him they had all 'tanked' themselves up a bit in the Jubilee. There was only one person that Danny was truly afraid of, either drunk or sober, and that was the eldest brother Jimmy. Jim had a fearsome reputation as a fighter. He was normally a very good-natured man who always had a joke to tell, but once he had 'gone' everybody knew it. His sight was very poor once his glasses were off, but if you had goaded him into 'fisticuffs' and he had actually, got hold of you then you were finished.

My big mouth was responsible for a terrible retribution on Danny and if time travel were possible I would very much like to go back and 'rub it all out'. The other brother, Uncle Con, had married a woman from Stepney called Alice. Now Alice was a very strong willed woman who would tolerate none of Danny's nonsense. I really liked Alice and was a frequent visitor to her house in Stepney for Sunday dinner. Danny could not stand her, probably because he could never intimidate her. Danny invariably knocked most of the family up when he was drunk, except Alice. Alice always told Danny that on the table by her front door she always kept an open pot of pepper and a knife. She said that the pepper was meant for his eyes and he'd find out where the knife was going if he ever knocked. Now Uncle Con was the quiet one of the family, although being of fiery Irish descent he could also handle himself in difficult situations.

There was a big family gathering, both in our house and Nan's house. Granddad, who was now quite deaf, asked me to pop up to the Jubilee and get his usual pint of mild and bitter. I collected the tankard and off I went. As I walked into the saloon Danny, who had not been invited to the family get-together, was standing there clearly well on the way to being drunk. There was the usual small man with the peaked cap on, who seemed to live in that very spot in the pub, crawling around and agreeing with everything Danny was saying. Clearly Danny was quite put out by not being invited to the 'do' and was being quite vocal about it. The pub was quite crowded this Saturday night and I just stood there, without acknowledging Danny, waiting to be served. Danny must have in some way blamed Alice for not being invited, because he suddenly grabbed me by the shoulder and shouted, "Do you know Connie's wife is a whore?" I did not reply, so Danny started shouting to all the drinkers in the pub that Uncle Con's wife was a whore.

When I had delivered the pint of mild and bitter to Granddad the party had moved into our house. They were all in the front room and upon entering Uncle Con asked if I got Granddads pint OK. I replied that I had and then foolishly said that Dan was making quite a scene in the pub, shouting out that Alice was a whore. Alice went berserk. What she was going do to Danny defied description. Uncle Con went very quiet and white faced. That was a bad sign. He kept going to our front door and looking down the street towards the Jubilee. Suddenly Danny came out of the Jubilee and started walking unsteadily down the street. Uncle Con came back in and told Alice that Danny was coming and 'leave it to him'. There was an immediate altercation just outside our house as Danny openly admitted the offence and fists were raised. Uncle Con swung a haymaker of a right-hander that landed squarely on Danny's jaw lifting him off his feet. He was probably unconscious before he hit the pavement. I was shocked, as I had never seen an adult punch up this close before. Mum whisked me indoors at the same time that Alice, allegedly, ran over to Danny's prostate body and removing her stiletto shoe proceeded to hit him around the head with it. I say 'allegedly', because I did not witness the attack, but as all the adults talked about it for some time afterwards so I'm sure that it must have happened.

The unconscious Danny was then carried into Nan's house and laid there for the rest of the night. I felt awful about what had happened and by lunchtime Sunday I went into Nan's house to apologise to Danny. Danny had now sobered up and was sitting by a large bowl of bloody water mopping his facial wounds. He did look a mess. There was one huge gash that ran from just above his eyebrow to the middle of his forehead, possibly caused as he hit the kerb when he fell from uncle Con's right-hander. The cut clearly needed stitches, but Danny was not the type to go to hospital. Smiling, he asked Nan to sew it up for him, but she wouldn't have any of it. I can assure you that Danny wasn't joking! He never did get the wound stitched and it just healed naturally, leaving an awful scar. Fortunately for me Danny had forgotten the events leading up to last nights fight and was only dimly aware of the fight with Con, which he entirely put down to Alice.

21

'It suits you sir.' – your back in the Club!

Late in 1959 I had finally saved up enough money for my Italian suit. I bought it 'ready to wear off the peg' from Granditers at Canning Town. It was a light grey three-button, single-breasted Prince of Wales check. The buttons were the fabric-covered type, to match the suit, and fourteen-inch bottom trousers. I also bought a pair of winkle-picker shoes with Cuban heels to go with them. That had cleared all my savings so I ordered two 14-inch neck white shirts with four separate 14½ inch starched collars from my tallyman, Mr Herbert and that was me sorted. I felt that I was the dog's bollocks and had now just started what was to become a lifetime obsession for clothes. Each month I would buy different style collars from either Granditers or Morris's tailors and weekly religiously take the collars to the Sussex laundry on the corner of Beaconsfield Road, Canning Town, to have them re-starched. By buying different style collars it looked as if you had a variety of different shirts. With care I could wear the rigidly starched collars for three days, so it was fairly cost effective. Not only that, but a proper starched collar looked so much better than the regular shirts with collars attached.

Also, I got my 'barnet' checked out. In the early 1950's Jack Monroe was the barber my mum took to me for a haircut at the West Silvertown parade of shops. Charley Allen was the other barber, but mum always preferred Jack Monroe. By 1959 Jack Monroe left the shop and so it was all down to Charlie Allen, who after showing me a number of hair models photographs suggested one he thought would suit my face. He was right and the new haircut was really great. With my new image, I was now really ready to get stuck in with the girls. I was now cutting Granddads hair as well, therefore he was also 'updated' with the 'Charlie Allen' special. There I was, dressed in 1959's height of fashion, with Italian suit and winkle-picker shoes all ready to get out and put it about. The only trouble was finding the girl! Well, I was by now back at the Drew Road School Adventurers Youth Club. Keen to get amongst the 'in crowd' in my new gear I returned to the Club to 'square it up' with the Warden. When I arrived in his office I started to tell him the story of how I was the innocent victim of a prank that led to me being 'banned'. Then it dawned on me that what with the new hairstyle and new clothes he did not even recognise me as the person he had banned. Previously I had a 'Marty Wilde' type hairstyle with a pulled down front quiff and a D.A. at the back and I also wore drainpipe trousers with a long jacket. Still, it was too late now, so I just sat there and explained how I was duped into entering his room in the same way that he was duped as to an intruder. When he remembered the incident he shook his head and said, "You still shouldn't have done it, but given the circumstances I'll give you another chance."

So, I was back in the club. It's amazing what a set of new clothes and change of hairstyle can do. All of a sudden one of the girls was saying that a friend of her's fancied me and why don't I ask her out. I did and she accepted. We agreed to go to the Woolwich Granada that Sunday afternoon. Her name was Brenda and she lived a couple of streets away from the club, in Lord Street. My dad knew her father, as he was involved in union work in Tate and Lyle. I arrived at her house at the agreed time Sunday afternoon and she seemed to have loads of brothers, because they kept on coming and going from the room I was waiting in. Also, her father seemed quite strict, asking what time would she be home, which was strange to me coming from an environment where no one ever checked on your comings and goings.

Considering that was about the first time I had really engaged myself in long conversations with Brenda we did get on quite well. There were no embarrassing long silences, with each of us thinking about what we could say next.

We arrived at the Woolwich Granada and from memory saw a horror film. I must admit that I cannot recall much of the film as I marched Brenda right to the back seats hoping to get stuck in to some serious 'snogging' as soon as possible. We leaned against each other and I sort of turned my face to her; she reciprocated and we were off. I must say that it was extremely enjoyable and went on for ages. Thinking back to my first 'boob squeeze', months earlier at North Woolwich Park, I thought that the time was right to indulge myself again and went for it. Although it was only over the top of clothing Brenda was having none of it and gently, but firmly, moved my hand away. I thought "You've blown it now, she's annoyed." I apologised. Brenda just looked at me, smiled, and said "That's OK" and we got back on with the snogging. I tried the same move again a bit later, but with the same result. I didn't say anything and neither did she, we just carried on smooching and I respected her for her stand. When we arrived back at her door we kissed very passionately for ages, locked in a very tight embrace. There was no more of me trying it on. We got so breathless that we had to walk around the block to calm down a bit. Then when we got back to her house we started up again. This certainly knocked the stuffing out of my prior encounters and when we finally parted we agreed on a date for the following week.

Now, unfortunately, the following week dad was removing our tiled surround fireplace and giving it to someone else. As it was very heavy he had counted on my help. I explained that I had arranged a date, but he was having none of it because he had arranged a set time for the person to collect it. I didn't find out until the Thursday and none of us had a telephone, so dad could not make contact with the person who was going to pick it up. I was well and truly lumbered and when you are that young you tend to be a bit laid back, not thinking about the other person's feelings. I let Brenda down and did not turn up for the date. I called around afterwards to apologise to her and when I knocked at her door it was her father who answered. If looks could kill then I was dead! I told him that I had called around to apologise to

Brenda and he started leading off at me. I thought, that's it, this is too heavy for me; I'm off!

Brenda came to the door and was quite nice and understanding about the situation. I apologised, because I felt awful about letting her down. I can recall how annoyed I was a year earlier when I had arranged to meet a school friend outside Woolworth's at Canning Town so that we could go to Poplar Swimming Baths together. He didn't turn up and I was furious. What I did to Brenda was worse! I really didn't feel that I wanted to get into a serious relationship and for all I know neither did Brenda. I just smiled at her and said that I would see her around the club.

Later, letting a girl down on a date did come back and bite me in the backside. I had been 'going out' with a girl who lived in North Woolwich for a week or so and arranged to take her out, to the cinema I believe. When the time came I just didn't fancy it and so I didn't turn up. This girl was quite different to Brenda; she was a complete extrovert and could get very boisterous. Very strong as well, I recall we had quite a few wrestling matches. Anyway, while I was out on one of my jaunts she came down to West Silvertown from North Woolwich to sort me out for standing her up. As I wasn't in she vented her anger on mum and when I returned home mum was furious. She said that if I was going out courting why can't I find a nice girl to bring home and introduce to her to the family. She said that she did not want to see any more angry girls on the doorstep making a lot of noise and swearing and that if I make a date then I must keep it.

22

Blown away by the miserable girl

It was around the first week in September 1959, being the last week of the six weeks school holidays. It was a weekday, early afternoon. I was all dressed up in my modern Italian gear and I think I was taking someone to the Woolwich Odeon cinema. Mum said, "You look nice." I smiled and said "Tat-ta" as I reached the front door. As I opened the door Mum shouted out, "Don't forget, find a nice girl and bring her home." As I slammed the street door I didn't realise just how close I was to that! I waited for the bus at the bus stop at the end of Westwood Road, just outside the café. Now, I was always an 'upstairs' person on buses. I never ever sat downstairs, but on this occasion it was almost as if a little voice in my head barked out an order 'downstairs today'. I jumped on the 669 bus and, reacting to the subliminal instruction, sat downstairs on the long seat next to where the conductor usually stands. I looked up and I was suddenly 'blown away' by the girl sitting opposite me. She was dressed in a long black coat, was wearing a headscarf and was surrounded by four large bags of shopping that almost took up the whole length of the bench seat. She looked nothing like the type of girls I would generally knock around with nowadays. She was not wearing any make-up at all and her face and forehead were shining, as if they had just been scrubbed with soap and water. She looked so miserable too. When I first looked at her there was a flash of déjà vu. It was very transient, almost subliminal, but something registered in my subconscious mind, as if the same voice had just whispered in my head, 'There she is.'

I sat there for a bit, trying not to make it too obvious that I was overly interested in her. I stared at her, she turned her head towards me and I turned my head away. This happened a few times. In fact, every time she became conscious of my staring at her she returned the stare and I looked away. Then I thought 'why not?' because faint heart never won a lady, so the next time our eyes met I gave her a big smile. A look of complete contempt came over her face and she closed her eyes at the same time as she turned her face away from me in an act of clear dismissal. I gave up and looked away, as clearly she wasn't as interested in me as I was in her. I say I gave up, but every time I saw in my peripheral vision she was not looking in my general direction I had another quick peep at her. When the bus arrived at the stop opposite Tate & Lyle, Thames Refinery, she struggled up with all those bags, that must have weighed a ton, and got off the bus. As the bus pulled away I looked back at her again, slightly puzzled as to why I was so interested in her and mentally trying to withdraw cupids arrow from my heart.

Around this time I also knocked around with Billy Smith from Knights Road. Violet and John Smith had four boys, Alan, Kenny, Billy and Ronnie and one daughter named Violet. Billy was my age and unfortunately, along with the youngest brother, Ronnie had caught polio some years earlier. Ronnie was lucky and came out of it unscathed, but Billy was left with a defect in one of his ankles, which left him with a limp. You will recall that the Smiths were great friends with mum who spent quite a lot of her evenings in their house. Billy and me used to go either to the cinema or swimming over North Woolwich Polytechnic Swimming Baths. After walking through the tunnel, or getting off the Woolwich ferry boat, on our return trip we would enter the phone booth by the pier, put our couple of pence into the meter and 'phone Billy's dad. Billy's dad would pick up the 'phone and say, "OK boy's I'm on my way." We would then press the button

'B' and get our money back. Ten minutes later John Smith would pull up in his Dormobile van outside the Pavilion public house and take us home. Our sole interest in films was either X-certificate horror films or films of a sexual nature.

I think that it was in December 1959 that I had an accident at school. It was during the metal work class when I was operating the lathe and I should have been wearing safety goggles. I accidentally turned the wrong lever and slithers of metal shot off of the piece of metal that I was cutting on the lathe. One piece hit me in the eye. I was in agony and rushed to Poplar Hospital. Fortunately it wasn't too serious, but I did have to be treated as an in-patient and wear a patch over my left eye for a week. It was during this week that Billy and me had planned to see a sexy film that portrayed a lot of nudity. This was a 'must' for Billy and me and, despite me only seeing it though one eye, we made the effort and went. I recall being a bit disappointed in the film, as I did not feel that it lived up to all the hype. It was about 8.00pm on Saturday night and I thought it was too early to go home. I told Billy that Mum, Dad and the rest of the family had gone to one of Tate & Lyle social evenings at the Tate Institute on the corner of Wythes Road. I never accompanied them to the Tate & Lyle socials during this period because they were at that particular time just not my type of thing. Nevertheless, despite having no tickets I felt a strange and overwhelming urge to go and see mum and dad at the social.

When we arrived at Tates Institute the Commissionaire on the door would not let us enter. I asked if he knew George Dyson and he said that he did. I wasn't surprised, as most people in T & L knew dad. I informed him that I was George Dyson's son and could he let dad know I wanted to see him. Dad came to the door and was really surprised to see me and even more surprised that I actually wanted to join them in the social and dance. As I sat at the table with the large group that mum and dad were sitting with I began to wonder what the hell I was doing there. My sister Kathleen kept asking me to dance with her, but I felt it was beneath my dignity to dance with a twelve-year-old. As I was looking around the hall and my head turned to the right hand corner of the hall I immediately knew why I was there. Sitting within a group, just two tables away, was the miserable looking girl I was so interested in a few months ago on the bus. I could not believe it.

I kept staring and staring and suddenly our eyes met. She knew who I was and looked away again. Now was my chance to show off my jiving skills. "Come on Kathy" I said, "let's have a dance." I don't think Kathy could believe her luck as she was up like a shot. There I was, very loud, all togged up in my best Italian style gear and, despite the patch over my eye, dancing for all I was worth. I kept looking in her direction and noticed that she was also looking in mine – along with her friends! I thought that maybe they were laughing at me, so I stopped the dancing and sat down. Anyway, it was getting late and Billy had to go home so we left.

23

Entering the 'swinging' Sixties

Also in 1959, the older boys from South West Ham Tech. were invited to the Plaistow Grammar Girls School dance. I was one of those lucky enough to be chosen to attend. We were all warned by our Headmaster, Mr Munden, that we represented the school and to be on our best behaviour. I must admit that I did feel a bit out of place there as I didn't go with anyone in particular; and didn't really fancy it because all the Plaistow Grammar girls I had met previously were a bit snooty. I just sort of walked around the dance hall and stood around with some of the SWHT boys who were one and two years older than me. Our School Captain was there, Colin Knight, who was two years older than me. In my year we all looked up to Colin, because he represented the school at boxing and had won the West Ham Championships. He also represented the school at chess. At fifteen years of age there is quite an appreciable gap between you and someone nearly two years older. In our year, given Colin's achievements, we all looked on him as a sort of school Super boy.

Suddenly, in the passageway outside the dance room there was a disturbance. Feeling quite bored I rushed towards the commotion. Some boys from Pretoria School were trying to 'gate-crash' our dance. Apparently, there was some prior 'bad blood' between Colin and these lads. I was surprised to see one of them shouting at, and shaping up to Colin. I thought he's in for a hiding and that it was all bravado on his part. Suddenly he struck out at Colin and they were fighting. They were rolling all over the floor and suddenly about half dozen of his mates ran up and started to put the boot into Colin's back and head. I found it quite sickening hearing the hollow thuds as their boots whacked into Colin's body. At this point I looked towards the dance room to see if any of the SWHT teachers in attendance were about to run out and break it all up. Far from it – in fact one of them who used to coach us in boxing was ensuring that the dance hall door was firmly shut. I could not believe it, just about the hardest teacher we had at school, who we all absolutely feared, was clearly seeing our schools prize pupil and captain being beaten up by a gang and was just closing the door! When I looked back all the kicking had stopped and the other boy was kneeling across Colin's chest, holding his arms down. He then head butted Colin a couple of times in the face. Then as quick as it all started it stopped and they all walked away from the scene. Colin had blood around his face and a huge bump on his forehead that looked like an egg had been implanted under his skin. I felt very guilty about not assisting Colin, but the gang of boys was also a couple of years older than me and I would have been slaughtered. I did not realise at the time that the repercussions of this night would catch up with me just over a year later.

Suddenly it was 1960 and on January 27th I reached the age of fifteen. This was to be a very eventful year for me. For a start I was walking alone from Silvertown Station to North Woolwich to meet with some friends in Woolwich Park. As I walked down the Albert Road I passed the building that doubled as the Conservative Club and Peggy Farrell School of Dancing on the corner of Leonard Street. Looking ahead I could see that miserable girl from the bus and Tate's dance again. Taking long strides, she was walking quickly towards me. I was in two minds whether or not to divert quickly down Leonard Street, but I thought that would be even more embarrassing than passing her now, with just a few feet between us along the Albert Road. I thought that I would carry on marching towards her and get a good look at her face as we passed each other. Initially, without looking at her face, I sort of eyed her body up and down and thought what a terrific slim figure she had. As we got to about six feet apart our eyes locked on each other. Neither of us smiled and now I was even more fascinated about her features and general appearance. I looked back as she passed me, but she didn't reciprocate. I noticed that she turned right, into Leonard Street and thought that she must be very local to there. She was clearly about my age and, given that I was by now a very frequent visitor to this part of Silvertown, I wondered why I had not seen more of her. I knew most of the local talent as they inevitably congregated in the Adventurers Youth Club, so why was this mystery girl never with the local 'in-crowd'? I carried on towards Woolwich and kicked myself for not being more forward. I felt that I should have at least smiled and said 'hello' to break the ice. I vowed that when I saw her next I would ask her out.

I also started knocking around with a new school friend called Dick. I had bought myself a Carlton 'Franco Suise' racing bicycle from Wag Bennett's at Canning Town. I recall that it cost me £32.00, which was a lot of money in those days. I frequently used it for the journey to school, depending on the weather. Generally Dick and I would just knock around with the rest of the crowd hanging about around the ice cream van that used to park outside the SWHT School entrance. This graduated to Dick coming around our house in Westwood Road one Saturday just to see our area and the crowd I hung around with. I remember how embarrassed I was when we returned to school on Monday and jokingly Dick started saying that Dyson's house was like a cave. I tried to laugh off but I was sort of hurt by the comments. I felt like whacking him on the nose, but you just can't do that to your friends and in any case he was only speaking the truth. We did live in very poor housing conditions. Still, things were looking up as we had been informed by the local council that we were all due to be moved into modern accommodation next year as our houses were being demolished under the slum clearance program.

Just after my 15th Birthday I was walking around Beresford Square, in Woolwich, when I saw a 'Robin Hood' hat in one of the tailors windows. They were in fashion at the time, so I went in and tried one on. I thought it looked great and course the shop assistant said that it really suited me. Well, he would say that wouldn't he? I was undecided on whether to buy it or not, because what looks good in your eye can look absolute rubbish in other people's eyes. So, I asked to try on some of the other hats in the shop, just to see how I felt I looked in them and to see what the shop assistant thought. Everything I tried on looked awful and the assistant was quite honest and said so. He said, "To be honest the 'Robin Hood' hat was made for you, it really looks great." I thought he was right and so I bought it. Everyone liked it, in fact a couple of mates on the strength of my hat, also bought one and looked complete idiots in them. So yes, it was made for me and stayed on my head until the summer of 1960, unless I was riding my bike of course.

Stupidly, I had now started to smoke. I first started when I went to another of Tate's socials with mum and dad. Now, 'social's' were not my type of thing, but I thought that I might have seen the 'miserable' girl again, but I didn't. I began to wonder where she might have been hiding. I had tried to make enquiries with some of the local girls, but had no luck whatsoever. They all said that they know of no such person and that she was probably visiting someone. Anyway, getting back onto the smoking I did not particularly enjoy it. Mum was quite OK with it though and always offered me one of hers at the social. I began to think that the socials were not too bad after all, because dad paid for all the drinks, mine being cider, and mum supplied the fags. It was a good free night out and gave me an excellent opportunity to hone up on my dancing skills.

I had started accompanying mum round to visit the Smith's in Knights Road, as I was also still knocking about with Billy Smith at the time. I really enjoyed the nights out in the Smiths, because it was very lively round there. John Smith was always cracking jokes and it was a very entertaining family atmosphere. John, I think, was an ex sergeant major in the army and worked as a security officer, or commissionaire, for a diamond importer in London. He used to bring home various bits of confectionery, or deserts, that were left after social functions and that was the first time I tried a crème brulee. Also, they had one of the new twenty four-inch super size televisions, so it was like being at the pictures. I remember the very first time that the new menthol cigarettes called 'Consulate' came out and Violet Smith gave me one to try. "Take it right down and hold the smoke in" they said, "it's really cold as it goes down your throat."

Silvertown Life

I did, and initially it tasted great, really cool and you could taste the menthol. I thought they were really good, as I had never inhaled the cigarette smoke like this before. I was halfway through my second one when I began to feel a bit nauseous. I walked into their garden and also felt very dizzy. I almost fell to the ground and started to vomit. Everything appeared to be gyrating and I felt very light headed. I lay on the ground in the Smith's garden for quite some time and needless to say I never tried a menthol cigarette again. Although it didn't stop me smoking completely, it certainly stopped me deep inhaling the smoke to that extent again.

My brother John was being given quite a hard time in Mr Davis's class, but not as bad a time as one of the Andrew's sisters from Eastwood Road was having. Apparently he was making her life hell. I felt that I just had to poke my nose in this matter that in fact really had absolutely nothing to do with me. I made a large 'Dunce's Hat' with a big capital 'D' on the front and underneath that I wrote 'For the man who terrorises children wear with Pride.' I then put it in a large paper bag and walked up to the school playground. I saw the Andrews girl, I believe her first name was Sally, and I asked her to give this bag to Mr Davis and tell him that it is a present from Stan Dyson. There was quite a furore over that prank. Mum never liked Mr Davis and although she laughed about the incident she said that I should not have become involved. I believe that the head mistress, Mrs Pearson, asked mum to see her, as Mr Davis, furious at what I had done made an official complaint. My prank resulted in him being even more difficult with my younger brother John to the extent that John started having nightmares about being in his class and did not want to go to school.

Mum decided that enough was enough and that she was going up the school to sort Mr Davis out. Generally, if mum had a complaint she would see Mrs Pearson, but given John's fear of going to school made mum flip and this was to be very, very personal. Aware of how nasty that he was to me seven years earlier and how I hated being in his class I wanted to accompany mum and register my dissatisfaction. Mum wouldn't have any of it and told me to keep my nose out of it. Mum put on her famous black raincoat and transformed into Batwoman again. Off she went, at full speed to the school with her cape flapping behind her. I decided that I was going anyway. I wanted to look as mature as possible, so quite immaturely I lit up one of my fags. Smoking away, I caught mum up just as she burst through Mr Davis's classroom door. Talk about Speed, Aggression, Surprise; this really was like an SAS raid. Mum rushed in shouting and clumped him. I followed in fast behind her hurtling expletives at him and inviting him to step outside and try and get tough with me now. He looked at me and shouted, "Put that cigarette out mister and get out of my classroom." I walked up to him, stared defiantly in his face and stubbed the cigarette out on his desk. He looked surprised and spluttered, "I'll have your GCE studies stopped for this." I continued my eyeball-to-eyeball with him and said "Try it!" followed by me inviting him again to step outside. With all the commotion Mrs Pearson then entered the room and asked me to leave and mum also gave me a push towards the door. I left feeling elated because I knew that I had come out on top and, as far as I was concerned given him his 'come-uppance'.

Having looked him right in the eye in this altercation and seen the reluctance in his eyes I had no further fear of him now. Therefore, whenever the opportunity arose, like him passing our street door on the way to the school, or me seeing him from the bus as it passed our shops, as I was going to school, I would shout an insult at him. He knew who it was and never ever responded in any way. I felt at last that I was giving some long overdue retaliation for my brother, sister and me, all of whom had suffered his bullying in his classroom.

24

Confrontation with the miserable girl

I had started knocking about with some girls in East Ham who lived in Greatfield Avenue and Lonsdale Avenue called Linda Painter and Beryl Warr. I forget how I originally met them, possibly over Tate & Lyle sports field, because Beryl's dad also worked at Tale & Lyle and knew my father quite well. They took me to one of their school dances, or it may have been a youth club dance, but the highlight of the evening for me was a great game of 'postman's knock' that ended with me having a good 'snog' in the darkened room with Linda. Originally, it was Beryl I was interested in taking out, but I ended up sort of going out with Linda.

I recall that on one journey to East Ham I had got off at the bus stop prior to Lonsdale Avenue and, as I came down the stairs of the bus, who should be sitting facing me on the bench seat downstairs but the 'miserable girl' with two friends. They all looked up at me at once. Outnumbered, I immediately looked away and jumped off the bus. As the bus drove off I had another look, only to see them all staring back at me laughing. I wondered if they were laughing at my Robin Hood hat, but I thought it was worth it just to see the miserable girl smiling for once. Clearly then, she was by now aware of my interest in her and had shared it with her two friends, who I recognised as being the same people from Tates social and dance night the prior December.

A week or so later, towards the end of May, I was with Linda and Brenda in Lonsdale Avenue. Some friends also accompanied me and we were all on our bicycles. We were having a laugh and I was quite enjoying myself when suddenly, for some unaccountable reason, an instant boredom hit me. I felt a bit uneasy, as I had a strong desire to go back to the Silvertown Station area. I whispered to my friends, suggesting that we leave, but they were having none of it, as they were enjoying themselves too much. The feeling would not go away, in fact it intensified to the point that I made a lame excuse to the girls and said to my friends "Are you coming or not?" The answer was clearly "Not!" I remember saying "Right, bye then, I'm off." I cycled away as if I was in a road race. As I cycled past Tate & Lyle's Manorway sports ground I had a quick look at it and recall thinking it will be a bit embarrassing when I see Beryl and Linda over there again, taking off as I did. Anyway, I sort of felt that I had 'blown it' now and that I would probably not see them again.

Peddling like mad I turned off the Albert Road into Leonard Street and then left at the bottom past Drew Road School. No one was about and by now I was wondering what on earth had possessed me to leave East Ham in such a hurry and what a mistake it had all been. I decided that I had completely wasted the evening and would cycle as quickly as I could back home to West Silvertown. I was just approaching Della Mura's shop on the corner of Drew Road and Andrew Street when I saw the miserable girl, quite alone and walking towards me. She must have just come out of Della Mura's. What timing! My Guardian Angel must have been really working overtime to plan this with such precision. I was going so fast that I had to brake sharp and skidded. She was certainly aware of my presence now, as I screeched to a halt about fifteen feet past her. All embarrassment was gone. A voice in my head said, 'Go for it!' I spun the bike around and cycled alongside her. I gave her my very best girl pulling chat up lines. Like a couple of low wolf whistles and a lot of clicking noises made out of the side of my mouth by my tongue, interspersed with squeaking noises made by pursing my lips together and sucking air back through my closed teeth, just like you would use

Silvertown Life

to call a cat. I was making a complete prick of myself! After an initial sideways glance at me the girl was taking all these male-mating calls with a quiet dignity, almost as if I wasn't there. My Guardian Angel, having worked so hard on this one, must have been sobbing as they watched me snatch defeat from the jaws of victory.

I maintained this childish charade all the way along the 400 yards of Drew Road, past the school and right into Leonard Street. She walked up to number 48. The last house before turning left into Newland Street. So that's where she lived, right next to Drew Road School and yet she had never been to the Adverturers Youth Club. I could not understand it, all this time searching for her and every night she was just yards from me. Anyway, now that I knew where she lived I cycled quickly back down to the corner, by the Wicket Gate café, and looking back I saw Virginia Lomas walking down Leonard Street towards me. Virginia was the daughter of Kath Lomas who owned the Off Licence on the corner of Parker Street and Drew Road. I waited for Virginia to arrive at the Wicket Gate Café and asked her who lived at number 48 Leonard Street. She told me that it was the Adams family, mostly girls, but she thought maybe one boy.

I enquired as to which one was about my age and when I described how slim she was Virginia said that it sounded like Joan Adams. I told Virginia if that is the one then I would like a date with her. I also enquired as to why Joan Adams never showed her face at the Adventurers Youth Club or mixed with the rest of the local talent. Virginia laughed and said she thought that there would be little chance of me getting a date with Joan, as the Adams girls were not 'out and about' type girls. She said "She's far too decent for you and really not your type." Nevertheless, I asked her to knock at the door and ask Joan if she would like to go out with me. I said that I would wait just on the corner, outside the Wicket Gate café, and if Joan were willing to go on a date then if Virginia waved to me I would then come over. I promised not to ride away and Virginia agreed to act as a 'middle-man' for me. As she knocked at the door I waited until it was evident that she was engaged in conversation with someone and then I jumped on my bike and rode away as quickly as I could. A bit later on, when I met Virginia outside of the Off Licence she told me she was annoyed that I rode away and would not tell me which of the Adams girls she had spoken to or what was said. I made my mind up that I had had enough of all this messing about and that the following evening I would knock at Joan's door anyway.

The following day as I approached Parker Street from Drew Road I was still unsure if I would have the courage to just knock. What kind of reception would I get anyway, because I had never spoken to the girl before, she seemed a bit unapproachable and I had made a complete 'balls-up' of all of my prior attempts. I was having this battle in my mind as to whether I would knock, or would not, when I turned the corner into Leonard Street and saw a younger girl I had frequently seen sitting on the wall outside the Adams house. She was sitting with a friend on the wall in front of one of the houses by the Wicket Gate café. I asked her if she was one of the Adams girls and she confirmed that she was. I asked her if Joan was in and she replied no, because she had gone to dressmaking evening classes in Plaistow. I told her to tell Joan that Stan Dyson would be knocking for her at about seven o' clock tomorrow and she just giggled and said that she would pass on the message. I was disappointed and at the same time relieved that Joan wasn't in and I wondered why I felt this nervous; it just wasn't like me. After chatting with various friends around the streets I caught the bus back to West Silvertown. I was about the only person sitting, unusually, downstairs once again. As the bus was going over the top of the viaduct, looking sideways to my right, I could see another bus was coming up the viaduct. Unseen hands turned my head, so that I was looking directly behind me as the other bus passed only to see Joan looking back at me from the other bus. I swung my head quickly to the left as the bus passed and she was still looking. "What a coincidence." I thought.

I believe that it was Wednesday 8th June 1960. Wearing the same Italian suit and winkle picker shoes that I had worn for school I set out at around 6.00pm for the short journey from West Silvertown to Silvertown Station. It was a lovely evening and as I was setting out earlier than I had anticipated I decided to walk. Anyway, walking gave me time to plan what I would or wouldn't say to Joan – if I actually plucked courage enough to knock on the door of this girl I had never exchanged words with, save for the mindless monologue I inflicted on her two days earlier. By 6.20pm I had arrived and was looking down Leonard Street. During the short journey I had acted out several responses after knocking at the door from a big kiss and 'why did it take you so long?' to 'Piss Off!' and the door being slammed in my face.

I stood by the Conservative Club for several minutes looking at the dock fence corner of Leonard Street and Newland Street where the Adams house was situated. I was now unsure if I could face my 'moment of truth' and actually knock. Last night, in bed, my supermind was kicking down the door, full of bravado. It's a pity we can't carry our supermind about with us during daylight hours. In the end I thought that I must get it over with as she can only say yes or no. After a few deep breaths I quickly marched down Leonard Street and into the porch of number forty-eight. I stopped dead in my tracks and was endeavouring to lift my right hand, which magically now weighed almost a ton, to grasp the knocker. I lifted the knocker, very slowly, and held it for a moment. No, I couldn't do it. This was far too difficult; all courage had deserted me and I was slowly replacing the knocker when the door was jerked away from me.

Suddenly there stood Joan. She was as surprised to see me, as I was to see her. We both let out a short Aaaagghh. Just like in the film E.T. when the young girl opens the cupboard and is face to face with the extra-terrestrial for the very first time. I said, "Hello, are you coming out?" Joan replied, "Yes, I'm just going round to the Off Licence." This consoled me a bit because it did cross my mind for a moment that she may be escaping prior to my threatened 7.00pm calling time. I continued, "Can I come?" Joan replied, "Yes, if you like." I said, "Did your sister give you the message about me knocking?" Joan gave a big grin and said, "You mean Patsy? Yes, she did." She had a wonderful face, lit up by that smile, nothing like the 'miserable' girl I thought she portrayed.

As Virginia Lomas had told me that the Adams girls are not the 'out and about' sorts. I said, "Did you mind me knocking?" She replied, "No, that's OK." We talked all the way to the Off Licence. Once inside, I got a big smile, raised eye browse and an understanding slight nod of the head from Virginia. I could almost hear her thinking 'Well, he made it then'. We talked all the way back to Joan's house and I waited briefly outside while she took in her purchases and we then walked and talked for miles.

Stan Dyson

Joan and Stan 1960

For me it was as if I had always known her and I really felt that I had found a soul mate. At the end of the evening we stood in her doorway. Now we had to get the difficult bit out of the way. There was no thought in my mind of passionate 'snogging' because I certainly didn't want to spoil the evening. I just looked at her and said "Is it OK if I come round tomorrow?" and Joan replied, "Yes." I responded "OK then, I'll call at about seven o' clock." There was a very pleasant kiss of about five second's duration and I departed. "Glad that that we got the first kiss out of the way" I thought as I walked towards the bus stop. For me that was it. As young as I was I really did have a very strong feeling that this was it. This was the start of my permanent life long relationship – and I wasn't wrong! There were no nights off for us, we saw each other constantly, did the same things night after night and never got bored with each other's company.

25

Getting involved in bad company

Back in West Silvertown, it was around this time that mum's long time friends the Smith's, from Knights Road, had a family crisis. I am sure that Violet Smith would have appreciated mums immediate help and support, but mum looked at it differently. Instead of mum calling on Vi and asking if there was anything she could do to help, mum waited to see if the Smiths made contact with her. Mum thought that to rush over would have been looked upon as an intrusion on their privacy and nosiness on mum's part. I think mum made the wrong decision here and for mum the long friendship with the Smith family ended.

It was around September 1960 that I was sitting in Michael Taylor's house at number 17 Westwood Road. Michael wasn't really one of my regular friends, although earlier in the year I had been accompanied him on a number of occasions when he visited much older youths it Mile End. Sometimes they would drive over to West Silvertown in a large black car and pick him up. They would drive very fast down our street and screech to a halt outside number 17, then Michael would jump in and they would race off again. Once, when he took me to visit his friends in Mile End, I was bundled in the black car and was joined by several more cars, all of which set off through Blackwall Tunnel in a 'convoy' to somewhere in Kent. I was handed a car starter handle and told this was my 'tool'. I asked what for and was told 'hitting with'. Apparently, this was a long time feud and the 'Mile End' boys were going to sort out the Maidstone boys at their local pub. I was Annoyed that Michael had not forewarned me about this, because I certainly wouldn't have gone. I had been involved in quite a few local scraps, but nothing like this. We were driving along country lanes at 70 miles per hour and I thought that any fight we got involved in would surely not be more frightening than this mad driving. Fortunately, the Maidstone boys were not in their local pub, they were probably looking for the Mile End boys in their local pub, and the whole thing just fizzled out. I never accompanied Michael to Mile End again.

Anyway, back to Michael's house in September 1960, we were the only one's in the house at the time when there was a knock at the door. Michael answered the knock and after a minute or two he called me to the door. He was having a heated discussion with two older youths, both of whom I recognised from the Plaistow Grammar School fight about nine months earlier. One was the assailant in the fight and the other had a supporting role as one of the 'kicker's'. It appeared that Michael had been speaking disrespectfully about them and they had come round to sort it out. One again Michael involved me and asked me to walk with them up to the corner by the Jubilee pub. I knew he wanted me as additional security in case they decided to sort him out there and then. I told them that I remembered them from the Plaistow Grammar School fight and they laughed and reminisced about it. Michael was endeavouring to talk his way out of the situation, but they were having none of it. They said 'we', and I don't know how I had now become involved, must have a meeting in Canning Town that evening. I said that I was courting and couldn't attend and they countered that by saying it would be a good idea if 'we' brought our girls because all the girls can have a chat while 'we' sort it out. I then got their backs even further up by saying that I couldn't bring my girl as she was very decent and wouldn't want to get involved in this mess. They then asked what I thought their girls were like then? Was I suggesting that they were not decent girls then? I managed to diplomatically extract myself from out of the hole I had just dug and then quite bluntly said that I was not involved in their dispute with Michael and did not wish to become involved in it, therefore I am now going back home. Michael hastily apologised for any misunderstandings and we walked back to our respective houses. Thankfully, courting Joan kept me out of further scrapes of this nature.

We moved into January 1961 and I reached the age of sixteen. I was studying for my GCE's and fast looking for my very first job, as I would leave school life behind me in July. I regularly went to the Sunday afternoon Church service at St Marks, next to Silvertown Station. The Vicar there was Reverend Joseph Stephens who was a friend of Joan's family. Joan had re-introduced me into attending church again, as I had not been since the earlier incident when the vicar at St Barnabus, West Silvertown, had frightened me off with his sex talk; however innocent he may have intended it to be it had put me off attending church. I was very keen to work for Tate and Lyle, Thames Refinery, and Rev. Stephens had business contacts there with the management. He suggested that I write in mentioning his name as a reference.

We were one of the first families to move under the slum clearance scheme in February 1961. We were moving to a modern three bedroom council house in Parker Street, Silvertown. This was better for dad, who worked in Tate's, Thames Refinery, as it was right at the end of Parker Street, and much better for me because I was then living just a few streets away from Joan. I was also very sad to leave Westwood Road because I had enjoyed such a wonderful and happy childhood there. I stood just inside our front doorway looking down the dingy passageway into the scullery. Thinking back to when I was really young and hiding from the coal man as he delivered one hundredweight sacks of coal by walking them halfway down the passage and tipping them, as best he could, into the cupboard storage space under the stairs. The noise of the coal tipping onto the floorboards sounded like thunder and the cloud of black coal dust erupted everywhere. George Hayward and Mr Burns were the names of the two West Silvertown coal men mum used in the 1950's. Can you just imagine these days, even the thought of someone walking into the middle of your house and shooting three hundred weight of coal and all the black coal dust into a cupboard?

I remembered back to when I was about 5-years of age, that mum asked me if I would be like a big man and shut the under stairs cupboard door up quickly after the coal man had shot his first load into the cupboard, just to minimise the huge cloud of coal dust settling everywhere. I think this had a dual purpose to stop me being afraid of the coalman and also getting me to sweep up all the coal dust that had settled over the long passageway linoleum floor covering afterwards. I had a long look at the scullery, and the stinking copper in the corner that I used to hide in as a kid. The winter wash downs in the freezing draughty scullery; standing in the luke-warm water with teeth chattering. I also remembered one of my favourite summertime jobs, being allowed to spray 'Flit' fly killer spray all around the kitchen at the flies. The Flit was poured into a small tin canister then the pump part was screwed on and when the pump handle was pushed in it created a fine spray of Flit that would zap all the flies. I used to be absolutely covered in the mist and my hair almost dripped with it. Flit was banned as an insecticide in the 1960's because it contained DDT, a poison that apparently never diluted away but just stayed in the environment, and your body!

I had a last look at my bedroom that I had taken such a pride in cleaning. I used to use Johnson's wax polish on the linoleum covered floor and spend ages applying layer upon layer of polish and buffing it up until you could almost see your reflection in it. I walked across the bedroom floor and looked into the glass-faced cabinet with my collection of 1957's very first Sputnik memorabilia and the model flying saucers I had made during this period. These items would be left in our old house as I was now past these childish things. I had a last look at the picture of Jesus Christ hanging on the wall over the central fireplace, with Christ holding a lantern up and knocking at a door. Nan gave it to me years earlier when I was in the St Barnabus Church choir and it was supposed to be a symbolic picture of Christ knocking on the door of your heart.

I also had a last look at the large, old fashioned, black polished sideboard that had always been in our downstairs middle living room, probably long before my birth. Mum always had her Phul Nana, California Poppy and Soire de Paris perfumes on one of its ledges. We stored all kinds of things in the hollowed out flange right very top of it. I used to hide under it as a kid and, as a toddler, my young brother John always used to run up the passage, trip over the linoleum in the doorway and fall right into the sharp edge of it. He almost had a permanent crease in his forehead! Tommy Batterbee acquired, and threw, the lighted matches across the room from that very sideboard and we all constantly used the large mirror fixed in the centre. I would miss all of those things.

26

Another family punch-up

Despite my prior nostalgic thoughts I settled very quickly into the new house at 44, Parker Street. It was nice to have a proper hallway, the coal fired central heating, large lounge, fitted kitchen, indoor toilet and at last a bathroom. I was very pleased that we had been re-housed in the area of our choice as many West Silvertown families had been moved to Canning Town and Custom House. I did not loose contact with my Nan and Granddad and some evenings Joan and I took the short journey back to West Silvertown to see them. It was during one of these visits that we fell foul of Danny.

We had just popped into see Nan and Granddad one evening and noticed that Danny was sitting in the middle living room with them. Due to misconduct he was not living with them when we left Westwood Road, but away from Mum's influence I guess Nan must have given Danny yet another chance. The atmosphere was very tense. Danny said to Nan "Tell them that I gave you some money for my keep today." Nan meekly smiled and nodded to me saying "Yes, he's been a good boy and given me some money today." Joan, looking at Danny quickly replied frostily "So you should pay for your keep if you're living here, there's nothing big in that." Danny went quiet for a moment then shouted at Joan, "Alright isn't it, when a bit of a kid comes in here telling you what to do." That did it for me! I screamed back "Don't you speak to my girl like that!" At the same time I tore off my jacket and threw it across the table. Danny shot bolt upright in surprise.

All I could see is a big red mist of anger in front of me for the way in which he had just spoken to Joan. Danny jumped up and ran around the table towards me and at the same time I raised my fists, ready for the punch-up. Danny ran right by me and out the living room door at the same time as I threw a right-hander, aimed at his head. It connected with the wooden door panel and the panel cracked. Full of adrenaline I didn't feel any pain. I heard the street door slam as Danny ran out of the house. Nan looked surprised, Granddad had a big smile all over his face and I was absolutely elated. Big Uncle Dan running away from me? I just couldn't believe it and really felt quite a man. Granddad said, "He was drunk earlier today and put a red hot poker to my face. I thought Granddad was just spinning a yarn, until I looked at his blue woollen jumper and saw the long scorch mark running across the shoulder.

About an hour later I asked Granddad if he wanted me to get him a pint of mild and bitter from the Jubilee. He confirmed that he did and I collected his tankard and walked up to the Jubilee. As I walked into the pub the small man wearing the cloth cap was in his usual position, just next to the bar. I was standing next to him waiting to be served when a strong hand grabbed my right wrist with a vice like grip. I looked to my right and it was Danny. Even worse, he was drunk! "Go home!" He shouted, "Go home!" I looked at him and said, "Let go Danny." Danny looked at me, and then turning to the crowd shouted, "I laid his father out, and he thinks I'm frightened of him?" The small man then said quietly in my ear "Stand your ground, boy, stand your ground.' Clearly he was just keen on prolonging the free entertainment. The tankard was, thank God, in my right hand that Danny was gripping. We were staring at each other and he looked very menacing and completely out of his head. My left arm was free and I considered punching him in the face, but then he was still my Uncle, and what if he just didn't feel it?

I pulled my right arm towards me and I swung my left arm around striking Danny with the palm of my hand hard in the chest. Danny fell back into the arms of the drinkers standing behind him. The landlord shouted across the bar at me "Out sonny, out! I didn't need to be asked to leave, and bolted out of the pub. I ran down to Nan's house and explained that Danny was now drunk and that it would be best if I left. Nan agreed and we hurried out of the house and back to 44 Parker Street.

I foolishly decided to chance my luck the following morning. I thought that I would catch Danny stone cold sober and that he would run out of the house again. Nan answered the door when I knocked and said, "No, don't come in Danny's here." I told her that it was OK I wasn't frightened of Danny and that I just wanted to check they were both alright. Nan beckoned me in and put her fingers to her lips. "Keep quiet then, Danny's asleep." Well, you couldn't keep quiet with Granddad because Granddad was deaf so you had to shout at Granddad otherwise he wouldn't hear a word that you were saying. Danny was lying stretched out in the armchair next to the fire and had probably been like that all night. The fire was quite low and I offered to stoke it up with some more firewood and coal. I brought the wood in the house to cut it by the grate. I was in a kneeling position by the grate, using a large carving knife to split the wood when Danny opened his eyes.

He looked down at me and rolled his eye's up. Blackbeard, the Pirate, came into my mind. Then a big smile came over his face and he stared down at me and said "You're trying to frighten me with that knife, aren't you?" I didn't answer, but just stared back at him. Again, still smiling in a menacing sort of way he repeated "You're trying to frighten me with that knife?" As he finished saying it his head was making small nodding movements, as if he were mentally confirming his own agreement with the statement. I responded, "I don't need a knife to frighten you Danny." With that Danny threw his head back and laughed out loud. At this point he looked almost possessed. He then gritted his teeth and screamed out very loud "I'll do him!" Then immediately looking down at me he screamed, "I'll do you, I'll do you!" I realised that Danny had not sobered up and that he was still quite drunk. Nan shouted, "Please go Stanley." I didn't need much asking as I was already on my way.

Quickly I returned again to Parker Street and I didn't mention a word to anyone about the incident. I didn't really want to get into an argument with Danny at all as I had always liked my Uncle Dan.

Silvertown Life

Outside of the booze he was great, but unfortunately Danny and booze just didn't mix. I did not see Danny for months after that incident, then one evening as Joan and I was walking down the Silvertown flyover towards Silvertown Station Danny passed us coming up. We both looked at each other full in the eyes, and then passed each other without acknowledgement or exchange of words. I always regretted that I did not stop and ask how he was, because really Danny was mentally ill with alcoholism.

27

Childhoods End

In July 1961 I left SWHT School and at the very young age of 16½-years I asked Joan's Dad if we could get engaged. It was a very embarrassing moment for me and I just blurted out all our plans to get married in September 1963. He laughed out loud and said that as far as he was concerned if we wanted to get engaged then we should go ahead and do it, so we did.

It was my ambition to start work in the accounts department at Tate & Lyle, Thames Refinery, but unfortunately there were no vacancies in July 1961. Back in the 1960's finding employment was so easy. You literally walked up to any of the factories from Tidal Basin right up to North Woolwich and their Personnel Department could sort you out with a job there and then. After breaking up from school I had a couple of weeks just lazing around, then, on walking out of Lyle Park, I called in at the nearest factory, Venesta Metal Containers Ltd which was right next door to the park. After a quick interview I was accepted as a costing office clerk and started work in August 1961. There were five of us in the Costing Office and we all smoked continually, in fact there was always a permanent haze of smoke; you didn't really need to light up a cigarette as it was sufficient just to inhale. Looking back I cannot believe how irresponsible I was during this period and why on earth they didn't just sack me.

One of the costing department assistants was called Dave Ritchie and I got on very well with him. He was a very intelligent and light-hearted person who was always joking about and was extremely helpful, and particularly patient in teaching me the job. He lived in Blackheath and used to come to work on a Lambretta Motor Scooter. He used to take me out for rides as the back seat passenger and one day was daft enough to show me how to operate the controls and let me ride it within the factory walls of Venesta's. After one rudimentary lesson I decided that I knew enough and, without his permission, borrowed it one lunchtime and drove it up to Canning Town. On the way back, with no crash helmet on, I had opened it to full throttle and was speeding down the viaduct towards the Victoria Dock entrance opposite Lyle's factory. Suddenly, ahead of me a long trailer lorry had pulled out of Victoria Dock and was doing a right hand turn towards Canning Town right across my path. I was going at such a speed that I could not think straight, so started to break. The scooter wobbled and skidded, so I stopped braking and flinched, waiting for the impact. I will never know how I missed the tail end of that trailer. As I rode the scooter into Venesta's factory gates Dave Ritchie was waiting for me. He gave me a long lecture about stealing other people's property and driving whilst uninsured. He said, "What if you had crashed the bike?" I shook my head and replied, "No problem, I was fine."

Dave always gave me first refusal on his 'surplus to requirement' items and I ended up buying a portable reel-to-reel tape recorder and a very powerful BSA Meteor .22 air rifle. Now, I was an absolute irresponsible menace with that air rifle. I still cannot believe that I used to take it to work with me and, leaning right out of the Costing Office window, fire pellets right across the North Woolwich Road at pigeon's sitting on the roof of Downeys Garage opposite. I'm also surprised that nobody standing at the bus stop opposite reported me to the police, as the pellets made quite a racket as they ricocheted off the corrugated iron roof. This was not the worse incident with the air rifle. We had two very reserved, and religious, Irish ladies who joined us as temporary staff sitting in the corner desks of the Costing Office.

I recall, almost in disbelief, that I went into the factory area and recovered three discarded, substandard, metal toothpaste tubes that had fallen off the production line. I then took them into the Costing Office and after removing three lever arch files from the wooden cubbyhole storage case and replaced them with the metal tubes. I loaded the rifle, at which point one of the ladies said, "Excuse me Stan, but you are joking here, aren't you?" Thinking nothing of it I just said "No" and pulled the trigger. Although it was only an air gun it did make a very loud 'crack' and an even louder noise when the pellet blasted through the back of the wooden cubby-hole and ricocheted off the wall. The Irish ladies both let out a simultaneous scream and ran out of the office.

I said, "Oh well, I suppose I'd better stop this now just in case they report me to personnel." They did report me and I were very nearly sacked. Harry Smith, the Personnel Manager, called me into his office and read me the riot act! He said that he should really sack me for this 'absolutely stupid' act, but that he would put it down to my complete immaturity in my very first juvenile employment and give me this very firm warning and a second, and final, chance. I actually felt at the time that they were the 'spoilsports' and that I had been unjustly treated. I was so put out by it that I walked down to the Graving Dock at lunchtime and enquired in Hollis Bros. Timber Merchants Ltd if they had any clerical jobs. The Sales Office Manager immediately interviewed me and confirmed he could start me the following week on a wage of £6. 10s. 6d. This was great because I was only earning £5. 17s. 6d. at Venesta's. At the end of the interview he said with a beaming smile "I've saved the best bit until last, because as a trainee sales clerk, as part of your apprenticeship, you will spend six months in Norway studying timber technology. He looked puzzled as he saw the look of horror and disappointment that crept across my face. "What's the matter then?" he said. I replied, "There's no chance of that because I've only just got engaged and couldn't go to Norway because I would miss my girlfriend too much. He just shook his head in puzzled disbelief and I returned to Venesta's Costing Office.

One good thing did come out of my short time working for Venesta's. One day there was a short practical program on smoking and lung cancer awareness, open to all the smokers who wished to attend. In our small office, with just seven staff including the two temps,

Stan with his dad in 1962 – the shed door is hidden just to the left

cigarettes were constantly on the go. As you entered the office from the outside you walked into a smoky haze. Sometimes, as I had nearly finished a cigarette, Dave Ritchie would open a packet of cigarettes and just toss one across the desk to me. I would then just pick it up and light it from the embers of my almost finished fag. The company nurse explained that as well as practical issues there would be a short film on the dangers of cigarette smoking. I was the only one in our smoke-infested office willing to attend. Dave Ritchie said that even if he attended it would not stop him smoking. I said, "Same here", but went anyway, because it was a break from the office tedium.. When I returned from the presentation I had about fifteen Peter Stuyvesant cigarettes left in my packet of twenty. I walked through the costing office door and, holding them up said, "Who wants them?" Dave said, "You can't have them back afterwards." I said, "I won't want them back" and I never ever smoked again.

28

Jobs Galore!

Although cigarettes were not as expensive then as they are today the money I saved smoking went into our post office savings book for our 'getting married' fund. Neither of us was earning very much in those days as I was 16 and Joan was 17 and in those days you got a 'rate for age wage'. We were saving like mad to hit our planned marriage date for September 1963. When I first met Joan in June 1960 she did not have a job. Her mother, Maude Adams, had died in February 1959 and Joan was forced to pack up school prematurely and take over the running of the house doing all the cooking, cleaning and washing for her father, Tom, and three sisters and brother. After a few months 'courting' I thought that she was being treated a bit like 'Cinderella' and that to enable us to start saving she would need to get a job. I don't think I was very popular with Joan's Dad for making that decision, but then it was a case of 'all hands to the wheel' and Joan's three sisters chipped in and they all shared the housework burden. Joan got a job in the staff restaurant at Tate & Lyle, just at the end of Leonard Street and was so successful in what she did that in a very short time she was promoted and given charge of the office pantry. We saved like mad and just walked and talked every night.

Some nights we would be walking through the Woolwich Tunnel into Powis Street and all around the Beresford Square area. Other nights we would walk down Cyprus Way to East Ham, or turn off just past Beckton Gas Works and walk down to Beckton Park then through the Connaught back to Silvertown for our usual nightly embrace in the doorway of 48 Leonard Street. Sometimes this could lead to embarrassing situations because if Joan's dad thought we had spent too much time in the porch doorway he would either shine a torch down the passage that we could clearly see through the glass in the door, or even worse creep up in the darkness and suddenly open the street door. Clearly, we needed more privacy.

Now, albeit that when he did just suddenly open the front door whilst we were in the passions of saying goodnight it was mildly embarrassing, the shed incident in my Parker Street house was probably our most embarrassing pre-marital 'goodnight' experience. Right alongside, and to the left, of our Parker Street main entrance door was the integral brick shed door. It was part of the house and had a Yale lock fitted. The right hand inside of it ran parallel to our hallway. It was stuffed with all our junk, including the Victorian mangle that for some unknown reason dad brought with us from Westwood Road. It always brought back bad memories for me of childhood times in our old scullery with me getting my fingers caught in the heavy wooden rollers. Many is the time I lost a finger nail there! There were two Yale keys to the shed door lock and they were always kept in an empty tobacco tin in the middle kitchen drawer, where most of dad's tools were randomly scattered. Sometimes the tin would open and the keys would fall into the jumble of tools, resulting in a frustrating search.

Now, Joan was a waitress in Tate & Lyle Thames Refinery staff canteen and she was also in charge of the Pantry that served all the offices. Joan was very popular and just before Christmas was inundated with Christmas presents from the office staff. Amongst these were lingerie presents some of the office girls said would be worth saving for our Wedding night – stuff the Wedding night, I wanted to see her wearing them now! As a lad a month away from his 17th Birthday, with his hormones out of control, I was fascinated by a sheer black nylon skimpy baby doll set Joan said she would save for our 'first night.' Suddenly I wanted the wedding brought forward! I asked when could I see her in this set? Joan, laughing, tormented me by saying that as soon as one of our houses was vacant. They were never vacant!

As I lay in bed that night it suddenly came to me – the shed. The following day I put it to Joan and she rejected it out of hand. 'There's no way I'm standing in that freezing shed in those', she said. 'You like them that much then you put them on and I'll look at you.' 'Anyway, if you think I'm going to stand there waiting for someone to come in and catch me dressed like that then your out of your mind.' The following day I started tidying up the shed and sorting out some heating. I bought half dozen night-lights, took both shed keys out of the kitchen drawer so that no one could enter, and left the night-lights burning for about an hour. When I walked back into the shed they had made no difference at all. It was still freezing. I started looking in the sideboard at the far end of the shed and bingo, there it was stuck at the back of the cupboard, dads paraffin blowlamp. I found some 'prickers' and cleaned out the nozzle and filled it up with paraffin for a trial run. I had used it before in Westwood Road helping dad strip paint off the doors and vaguely remembered that once you had pumped it up and set it roaring then you had to maintain the pressure because if it dropped off too much it ceased to be a blowlamp and became more like a flame thrower.

It worked! You first had to place some small bits of paraffin soaked rag in the recessed area at the top and set light to them so that they heated the tube to the point that it vaporised the paraffin. It smoked like mad and you could almost hear the roar of it through the wall in our hallway, but it did heat up the shed – a bit! I explained it to Joan and she was distinctly nervous about the whole thing, but clearly I was a man on a mission and she was sympathetic and probably quite flattered that I was so keen to see her in these flimsies. I explained that it would all work out fine, as I'll take both shed keys and bend one slightly so that it will not fit the lock, that way we won't be caught. In the unlikely event that someone wanted to go into the shed at 10.00pm then seeing that the key won't fit they would go back and search amongst the tools drawer for the other missing key, giving us time to escape. Joan was clearly uneasy about the whole set-up, but for the sake of a quite life and to get this male fantasy over, she agreed.

I'd been in and out of the shed from 9.30pm onwards making sure the blowlamp was OK and Joan said her goodnights to all at 10.00pm and we left the house. As soon as I opened the shed door Joan said, 'Why are all these candles burning?' I explained that I had checked it out previously and when it's dark you can see a chink of light through the side of the shed door when the electric light is on. She shook her head, and said, 'Anyway, it stinks in here, what's that burning smell?' I said it's OK because I had put the blowlamp out about 5-minutes earlier. 'What's that dirty old camel coat doing laying across the floor?' 'You're not expecting me to lay on that are you?' Blimey, this was like a cross between '20 Questions' and 'What's my Line?' I had taken the old camel coat off the hanger in the hallway, where it had been stuck on a coat hanger since we moved into the house to distract from the coldness of the concrete floor. It was the same camel 'great coat' that used to hang, for as long as I can remember, on a hook at the back of the middle room door in Westwood Road and I'm sure that at one time it must of hung on dad's shoulders in Germany in WW2. The thought of Joan laying on it had not crossed my mind – in your dreams!

Well, we finally got around to Joan trying on the objects of my desire. 'I'll close my eye's, I said. 'Why' said Joan? 'Well', I said, 'I'd rather see you when you're ready.' 'Ready for what?' said Joan, 'don't you think I'm messing about in here, I'm nervous enough just being in here dressed like this.' 'Right', she said. I opened my eyes and wow, she looked absolutely gorgeous. I took hold of her and we leaned against the shed wall. 'No!' said Joan. I kissed her and I could feel her relaxing already. At which point we heard raised voices through the wall. Mum and dad had started to have a row. It was a bit off putting, but I was ready to stay the course until, quite loudly, through the wall we heard dad shouting in the hallway, just about a foot away from us, 'Where is it then woman? It's not under the stairs and it's not in the passage!' Mum shrieked back, 'Then it must be in the shed!'

Well, Joan went stiff and looked just like a rabbit caught in car headlights. Now I'd done it. Here she was, dressed up like something off the Christmas tree and had now gone completely catatonic on me. 'Don't worry', I whispered, 'He can't get in I've bent the key. He'll start looking for the other one.' Suddenly it was like an old 'Keystone Cops' movie; everything was on 'fast forward' for us, well for Joan it was as she struggled to get fully dressed again. Then we heard the street door open and a key go into the shed door lock. It was jangled about a bit then dad shouted 'Fuck it!' It was as much as I could do not to laugh – my plan had worked just fine. The front door closed and dad shouted out as he walked down the hallway, 'Bloody fool woman, you've bent the key in the lock.'

Joan was now fully dressed, the gossamer baby doll lingerie, that would probably have fitted quite easily into an envelope had been tucked away somewhere and we were ready to make our getaway. Slowly, I opened the shed door and looked into the darkness of our porch. Now, I was aware of the situation that dad may at any moment put in an appearance and, unfortunately for dad, he did not share the same intelligence. The front door was just over a bricks width away from me as I peeped my head out of the shed and was immediately eyeball to eyeball with dad bursting through our front door. We almost nutted each other! Although, I was marginally prepared for the situation dad was not. I let out a slightly startled 'Aagh', but dad, suddenly confronted by this completely unexpected face-to-face meeting with a shadowy figure in the dark let out a very loud 'Aaaarrrggghhh!!!' and leaped backwards so quickly it's a wonder he didn't break his back.

I said, 'It's all right dad, it's me.' Clutching at his chest he replied, 'you stupid bastard, you frightened the life out of me! What are you doing in there?' 'Just saying goodnight to Joan.' I replied. Dad, still quite breathless from the shock said, 'What's that burning smell?' He turned on the shed light and looking down said, 'and what's my coat doing on the floor?' Clearly, in the eight years mum and dad were courting they didn't get up to much hanky-panky then? He then said, 'was it you who bent the key?' Dad had not fallen in with my plan of searching through the tools for the other key and had just used two pairs of pliers to straighten the bent one. That's why he was so quick. At this point, with all the commotion, mum appeared on the scene. 'What's the matter?' she said. Joan and I just looked at her, and then sniffing the air she said, 'Has someone lit a fire?'

It was quite some time before Joan recovered from the embarrassment of that evening and we could laugh about it. I still have dads old fashioned paraffin blowlamp today and whenever I am tiding out the garage and pull it out from the back of the cupboard I hold it fondly, as I am mentally transported back through the years to the shed.

In January 1962 I wrote to Tate and Lyle again, still desperate to get a job there, but I was very disappointed to receive a letter on Monday 29th January stating that they had no suitable vacancies. On Sunday 4th February 1962 Reverend Stephens told me to write a letter to Silvertown Services Lighterage Ltd, who were the shipping and lighterage subsidiary of Tate & Lyle, and with a smile winked at me. I thought that good old Reverend Stephens, who was the spitting image of the actor Jimmy Hanley, must have pulled a few strings for me and I immediately wrote a letter of enquiry about employment. Silvertown Services Lighterage Ltd were situated right next door to The Ram public house, opposite where Granddad lived in 1912 at number 3 North Woolwich Road, prior to the demolition of the terraced houses in 1934 to make way for the Silvertown Viaduct.

I went for an interview at Silvertown Services on Wednesday 14th February and got the job as a bought ledger clerk. I started working for them on Monday 26th February 1962 and I was over the moon, working for Tate & Lyle at last. Also, it was nice to be still working in my beloved West Silvertown, with the familiar factory smells and I was also still able to shop in my favourite parade of shops and chat to the old shopkeepers who had known me as a schoolboy, before I started work. Mick and Alf Knightley in their sweet shop, Ted Manning in his fish shop, Jean Docherty in her Newsagents who I worked for as a paperboy. Next to Jean Docherty's Newsagents there was Mr Scott, in the Post Office that he had run for years and finally John Pattison and his mother Kate in the Grocery and Greengrocery shops who I had worked for just a couple of years earlier as a school kid. It was really great to still be in touch with them on a day-to-day basis because other mates of mine had been forced to catch buses and trains into the City to gain suitable employment.

29

Finding somewhere to live

Nan and Granddad had been re-housed into a ground floor flat in Balaam Street, just past the swimming baths and before you reach the sewer. We had been around to see them in their new flat and Danny was living with them. I believe he slept on the settee, because it was only a one bedroom flat. He was 'off the drink' and extremely pleasant, more as I remembered him when I was a kid in the early 1950's. It was one Saturday in summer 1962 that we bumped into John and Florrie Jordan in Woolworth's store in Canning Town. Joan knew John from working in Tate & Lyle. We were talking to them about our wedding plans and they asked where we would be living after we got married. We really hadn't got a clue. They told us about Mr Marsh who owns a lot of property and sits in a chair all day in the shop at the back of Silvertown Post Office. They said that they were now living in one of his flats, in effect a converted house with a shared front door. "Great" I said, "I'll go and see him."

The following day we went into the shop at the back of the Silvertown Post Office and sure enough, there was this very elderly man just sitting in a chair. I walked up and asked if he were Mr Marsh. He confirmed that he was and I explained that we were getting married in September next year and we would like to go on his property rental books. He immediately handed us over to Mr and Mrs Barton, who looked after the shop and his property business for him. I immediately clicked with Mrs Barton. She was a tall blonde, quite good-looking woman around mid forties. She took our details and explained to me that Mr Marsh also had a 'furniture book' and that it was 'helpful' and you would be 'prioritised', if you paid money into this fund.

She said that it was all good quality furniture from Harris Lebus main store in Central London. To me it was quite clear that the more money you had invested with them the better chance of a good property rental, so we transferred about five hundred pounds across from our Post Office savings account into their furniture account. As the weeks passed we added further money to the 'furniture fund' and this paid off, because my mum told me that Mrs Barton would like to see me. Joan and I called in the shop and Mr and Mrs Barton explained that one of the best 'self contained' flats was becoming vacant. It was number 394 Albert Road, right opposite Loders & Nucoline, and that although we were not getting married until September 1963 if we wanted it and one of us was prepared to move into the flat in January then it was ours. They explained that their Son was currently living in the flat, but that he was shortly due to vacate it. "Just one small problem" said Mr Barton, the Wyatt's from North Woolwich also want the flat and they have offered £100.00 as 'key money'. We won't take key money, but there is £100.00's worth of fixtures in the flat.

I could not believe our luck. We viewed the flat on 12th January 1963 and it was great, especially being 'self contained' and having your own front door and back garden. Also, we could have as much sex as we liked! No more getting caught out by dad in shed situated right next to the front door of our house. No more long walks to Abbey Woods, getting covered in dirt and leaf droppings and having some nosy bugger spying through the bushes at you. Never again would either the Lomas's in the Off-Licence opposite our house, or any of the other neighbours wonder what on earth I was doing every Saturday at around three o' clock in the afternoon.

On Saturdays, just before 3.00pm, Joan would come round our house for a bath. I would say, in quite a loud voice for all to hear, "I'll run your bath water and then I'm off round the shops." After running the water I would make a play of walking into the lounge and saying,

Stan and Joan outside their first home at 394 Albert Road Silvertown in summer 1963

"Bath waters ready Joan and I'll see you later, if I'm not back then I'll see you tonight." Joan would go upstairs for her bath and I would shout out "I'm off mum" loudly closing the street door. I would then walk down our path, open the gate, then turn right and after four paces, which took me out of sight of anyone sitting in the lounge, I would climb over our the front iron fence that bordered the Doran's house next door and into our front garden.

Once in the front garden I would put one foot on the top of next doors fence and then lift myself up so that my hands were on the top of our extended porch. I would then climb onto the porch and then climb up through my sisters bedroom window, which I always ensured was open, through her bedroom and after seeing that the way was clear I would then tiptoe across the landing and do a coded tap on the bathroom door. Joan would open the door and I was in. We would share the luxury of a bath together, and other activities, after which I would peep through the bathroom door and if the way was clear then I would retrace my steps through the front window onto the roof of the porch and drop down into our front garden. Then after climbing over the small fence into the street I would take four paces right, open the gate, up the path and knock on the street door. Funny, whoever answered the street door, always said, "Why don't you take your key?" We were never caught! We did have some near misses though. Remember that this was over 40 years ago and attitudes to pre-marital sex were quite different to the tolerance of today. If then were now, what would I have said?" "Mum, I'm just off up stairs to have a bath and sex with Joan – see that we're not disturbed, won't you?"

The year 1963 was a very eventful year for us. That was the time when it started snowing on Boxing Day 1962 and didn't finish for weeks. We really were 'snowed in' at the start of 1963. At last I was due to finally leave home and move into the flat in January. What would mum do without my weekly house keeping money? Even when I was just a few years younger mum liked to ensure that I contributed my 'whack'. I recall that even at that time, still at school and with all those jobs, when I went on a weeks holiday mum asked for 'my keep'. "What's that for?" I said, "I'm away." Mum replied "It's to keep your bed open while you're away." Who on earth was going to want to move into a seven-day tenancy agreement in an East London boy's slum bedroom whilst he was away on a well-deserved weeks holiday?

In January we had paid the £100.00 for the 'fixtures' and had I known how short a time we were going to stay in the flat would I still have paid it? You bet I would, because although our tenancy was short we had a terrific time and later it was a great start to our married life. Dad said that it was 'key money' but so what? We really had no choice because we needed somewhere to live and the position of the flat, and the fact that it was self-contained was great. Although, at the time £100.00 was equivalent to about fourteen weeks of my gross wages! When we bumped into Florrie and Johnnie Jordan again later in the year, they were a bit surprised that they recommended us to Marshes Property and we ended up with a prestigious self-contained flat. On Thursday 24th January we went to Harris Lebus in Central London and chose out furniture. On Friday 1st February 1993 I 'moved in' with just two pillows and in the dining room, in front of a roaring fire, we immediately proceeded to 'christen' the flat.

30

'Goodbye Granddad'

We also had a sad time in February 1963. Granddad had become very senile and was dying. The double bed had been moved out of his bedroom and into the lounge. Most of the time he was almost incomprehensible, slipping in and out of consciousness. Mum said that the priest was going to see him and give him the last rites. Joan and I hurried over to see him on Sunday 17th February, but really I should have gone sooner. Granddad was laying flat out on the double bed in the living room. Danny, Nan and the Priest were there. I tried to speak to Granddad, but most of the time he was unconscious. When he was conscious he just spoke gibberish. I stayed for a long time and when the Priest left I told Nan that I would stay until he regained consciousness again, say my last goodbye and leave.

I walked over to Granddad and sat on the bed. I called him, but there was no response. I think it was Danny who said that he would lift Granddad up a bit and stick some pillows under his back. During the course of the lifting Granddad opened his eyes and looked at Danny. Again, I sat on the bed and started talking to him, about the old days and the good times we had together. All the times I pestered and tormented him. It was hopeless, I don't even think he knew who I was, it was like the lights were on but no one was home. I said to Nan, "I'll have to go now Nan, he doesn't even know who I am." Nan agreed.

I looked at him, propped up there and said, "I wished I'd have come sooner to say goodbye properly." Nan had tears in her eyes. I said goodbye to Nan opened the door and then took one last look back at Granddad. I then said "Goodbye Granddad." He was looking at me straight in the eyes and he lifted his arm slightly, pointing at me and said, "Thrupence, ice cream." I couldn't believe it, he had gone back in time to the early 1950's when he was the pot-man at the Jubilee pub and I used to bang on the Pub window pestering him for three pence for an ice cream. The look in his eyes changed, as if he had suddenly become lucid again and he said "Goodbye Stan." For a moment I was dumbfounded. He then said to me "Shut the biscuit." Clearly he meant the door, but he was off again and immediately lapsed into gibberish. I left content that we had said our last goodbye and Granddad died three days later on 20th February 1963.

Nan was now left to share the flat with Danny. It wasn't long before he was back into his drinking ways again. By now he would drink anything to feed his alcoholism, including methylated spirits. Nan discovered many bottles of it stored in one of the high cupboards she never generally used. Nan said that one night Danny came into her bedroom and sat on her bed talking to her, clearly drunk. She ordered him out of her bedroom and she said that he then placed a pillow over her head, presumably with a view to suffocate her. She managed to struggle free and I believe she may have ran around to her son Jimmy Guinee, who lived in Chesterton Terrace, Plaistow, which was really just the next exit along the sewer bank. Danny had long since gone when Jimmy arrived at the flat, but Jimmy knew that Danny would be back.

When Danny returned and knocked at the door of Nan's flat Jimmy was waiting. When the police arrived, on seeing the state of Danny, who was just lying semi-conscious on the steps outside the flat in Balaam Street, they asked if a car had hit him. Jimmy said, no it was him and went on to relate what had happened to Nan and that upon his return, fuelled by the alcohol, Danny made the mistake of squaring up to Jimmy. Danny was taken to hospital and as far as the police were concerned that was the end of the matter. A clear case of self defence

Silvertown Life

and unlike the political correctness of today where the intended victim is arrested for using undue force in defending themselves. Oh, to return to those days of common sense again! Danny never returned to Nan's flat again and some weeks later was found lying on a building site in Stepney. It would appear that in one of his drunken states he had been seriously beaten up and he died of his injuries in hospital.

I was enjoying my working life at Silvertown Services Lighterage. Most lunch times were spent playing table tennis in one of the large hangers in which the barges were repaired. Ralph Daniels, the Accounts Manager, had introduced me to table tennis, a sport I had never played before, and I really took to it like a duck to water. I ended up representing the Tate and Lyle 1st team in both the Barking league and Silvertown and District Business Houses league. Ralph also introduced me to photography and suggested that I buy a 'Werra' 35mm camera. This gave me the opportunity to take some photographs of West Silvertown School and Westwood Road during lunchtimes. The snow was still on the ground but, unfortunately, by then all the terraced houses in Westwood Road had been demolished. Too late again Dyson!

31

Married life and family planning

The Reverend Stephens married us, at St Marks Church, Silvertown, on the 7th September 1963. We had a great reception in the Co-operative Hall, Kennard Street, which was just around the corner from our 394 Albert Road flat, and an even greater first night together. We had never actually slept together all night and in the three years that we had been courting we had been really careful with contraception. It was all condoms and Rendells Pessaries. There was no contraceptive pill in those days, so Joan had been to Stratford family planning clinic and been fitted with a contraceptive cap. We completely threw caution to the wind, on our 'first night' together and used no contraception at all. The rest of the month Joan struggled with the cap and contraceptive cream. Our Daughter, Joanne, was born nine months later in June 1964.

I really enjoyed the company of my colleagues at Silvertown Services Lighterage, especially the lunchtime drinks in The Ram, the lunch time table tennis and the great time we had on the Sugar Line ships when they berthed right outside our office building that was situated right on the edge of the River Thames. The Purser and Stewards had all sorts of

Stan & Joan get married on 7th September 1963

goodies they brought from the West Indies, and probably other Ports, which they used to sell to us on the cheap. Although they certainly didn't do as much trade as Len Bull, who was in charge of the Yard Gang and did a rip roaring trade in cut price Durex contraceptives.

Unfortunately, I did not really fit in with their outdated system of management and found it quite difficult to call the General Office Manager, Mr Caton, 'Sir', as most others did. I suppose, in a way because of my attitude that was one of the reasons why I did not get an annual salary increase in December 1963. There were only two of us in the entire staff that didn't get a rise that year. The Director, Mr Collard, used to call staff in randomly to his office, from different sections within the complex, that way you never knew who would be next to hear their salary increase. Once it got down to the last half dozen you would get quite self conscious about it, because everyone knew you hadn't been called yet. I found this quite humiliating and decided that after Christmas I would find a new job.

It really was just a case of walking down the North Woolwich Road and calling at the front reception of each company. There were no jobs next door at Pinchin Johnsons and given the awful smell I just could not face working in John Knights soap factory. I had already worked at Venesta's, so the next port of call was Silcocks Animal Feed. I was successful in getting a clerical job in their general office and in January 1964 I walked into Mr Catons office to hand my notice in. I was all ready to have a 'big barnie' if he started to get funny over the situation. When I gave him my one weeks notice and told him I was going to Silcocks he looked quite shocked, because nobody ever left Silvertown Services. He said, "So you think they can offer you better prospects than us, do you?" I replied sharply, "Not only better prospects, but a lot more money." He just dropped his head and said, "Ok, can I have it in writing please." I walked out of his office and started work at Silcocks the following week.

Silcocks was so 'laid back' and informal compared with Silvertown Services, and very friendly, but how I missed those excellent free staff three course meals we used to have at lunchtime. Silcocks was also situated right on the Thames and had a berthing area for boats to load and unload animal feed. There was a huge underground storage complex for all the different substances and antibiotics that went into the animal feed and also thousands of sacks of the finished product. Given that you were situated right on the bank of the Thames and the very nature of the product, talk about 'Rats, Rats as big as Tommy Cats in the Stores' because that underground stores complex was not a place for those of nervous disposition. I spent a lot of time in that area and quite enjoyed it.

Joan was taken into Howards Road Hospital, Plaistow, on Thursday 25th June 1964, as she was 'overdue' and they broke her water the same day. Our Daughter, Joanne Helen, was born at 11.30pm on Sunday 28th June 1964. I didn't have a car then, only the Carlton Franco Suise bicycle and when, after phoning the Hospital at 10.00pm. they told me she was in the labour ward I cycled from Silvertown to Plaistow and created quite a disturbance when they refused to let me in to see her. In the end they agreed to let both me and my bike in, and I saw Joanne just moments after she was born. It was well past midnight when I left the Hospital and I spent the next hour cycling around to Stratford, Canning Town and other addresses in Silvertown to let the rest of the family know about our daughters birth. I did not go into work the following day, because not only was I exhausted, but also

I wanted to get up to the hospital and see Joan and Joanne again. I 'phoned Silcocks and left a message about my absence, saying that I would take it as a day's holiday. What a fuss the Office Manager made the following day. We really fell out over this one! His opinion was that your Wife having a baby was quite a minor excuse for taking a day off, albeit that it was a holiday, because nothing was more important than your job. I can still see the shocked expression on his face when I told him that nothing was as important to me as my family and that if that's the way he feels then he can 'stick' his job.

A couple of months later, when we were shopping in Rathbone Street we bumped into Florrie and John Jordan again. Florrie said that they hoped to move out of their flat because she was now working for Standard Telephones and Cables Ltd and they were transferring a large portion of their workforce to their new factory in Basildon, Essex. She said that brand new accommodation was being given to all STC employees by the Basildon Development Corporation and although you may need to travel from STC in North Woolwich to STC Basildon and back each day, the coach travel was free. She said that they hoped to get a two-bedroom house or failing that a maisonette.

That evening Joan and I discussed whether it would be a good idea for us to try and move to Basildon, because based on what had already happened to Joan's sister, when we were re-housed by the council the best we would probably get is high rise flat accommodation. I decided to give it a try, as Standard Telephones was literally just across the railway lines opposite, just 400 yards from where we lived. I walked across the Railway Bridge and asked at STC main gate whether they had any office vacancies. The security man said they did not have any vacancies for office staff at all. As I was walking away he shouted, "Unless you want to move to Basildon."

Apparently many local people didn't fancy the move and they were on a recruitment drive to replace certain key office staff. Their Basildon Personnel Manager, Stan Yates, conducted my 'Basildon' interview. After completing the job application form Stan reviewed the content. It did not look very promising. Shaking his head Stan said, "You see, we are looking for an experienced Export Invoicing Clerk and you haven't any experience at all in that field. Then, just as I had given up hope he turned to the last page that detailed interests, sports and hobbies.

His face lit up and he said, "You play Table Tennis then?" I had become quite an accomplished player by then and I replied, "Yes, and I won both the Handicap singles and was part of the winning team in the Silvertown and District Business Houses league earlier this year." What I didn't know at the time was that Stan was the STC Table Tennis Secretary. Stan continued, "Would you be able to play for us this coming season in the Silvertown Business Houses and also the Barking League?" "Yes, I would." I replied. Stan smiled and said, "Let me see what I can do." He went away for some time then he returned and introduced me to the Jack Wilson, the Billing Department Manager. One week later I started work as an Export Billing Clerk at Standard Telephones and Cables and also as a regular member of their Table Tennis Team.

STC North Woolwich was a great place to work. Not only was it a 'fun place', almost like being back at school, but also it was only just across the road from where I lived. Also, there was plenty of 'overtime' that this nineteen-year-old breadwinner really needed to help out with the family finances. Three months later my department transferred to Basildon and I had to endure a daily free return coach journey to Basildon. On the very first day, as I boarded the coach I saw Florrie Jordan again. She said that she had been travelling for about four months and was hoping to be accommodated in Basildon soon. Stan Yates told me that he had put me down as a 'key worker' and that generally they were given accommodation priority. After three weeks of coach travel we were given a brand new three bedroom council house and on Monday 21st December 1964 I finally left my beloved Silvertown and moved to Basildon

32

New life in Basildon

Initially, for us, it was a bit of a culture shock. Although the house was lovely we found it hard to settle in Basildon. Every weekend we would get on the train at Laindon Station and we heaved a sigh of relief as we moved past Barking Station and started to see the familiar dark and dingy Victorian terraced houses again. We had been extremely lucky though, in getting such good accommodation so quickly. Florrie was dismayed and she just could not understand how I was fitted into a new 3-bedroom house so quickly, because she had to travel for a further few months before she was given a flat. Just goes to show that sometimes it isn't what you know, but more a case of whom you know. Nevertheless, it all worked out OK for Florrie and Johnnie in the end, because many years later they moved into a four-bedroom house in our street where they still live in 2004.

We have had a very successful life in Basildon. The 3-bedroom council house is long gone and we live in a nice detached house in Laindon, Essex. In August 2003, at the age of 58, I took early retirement after having over 30 years experience working in the field of credit management. I now work just a day or so each month conducting seminars in credit management and county court litigation across the

UK. Our Daughter Joanne lives about half mile away in Langdon Hills and we have four wonderful grandchildren.

We do still visit West Silvertown, generally about three times a year. It is still a very special place to me, but it has now changed almost beyond recognition. The only original houses left in West Silvertown in 2004 are those in Boxley Street, Bradfield Road and some of Mill Road. The two small groups of houses that originally housed senior workers connected to Lyles factory in both Evelyn Road and Hanameel Street also still survive. The huge landmark factory of Tate & Lyle Plaistow Wharf has now been demolished. The docks have disappeared, being now just a valley of water flowing into the Thames, surrounded by maisonettes and blocks of flats. Perhaps to the younger generation of today this is progress and they will look back with fondness to their West Silvertown life in 2004, just as I do to mine in the 1950's.

Remembering West Silvertown life, as it was in the 1940's to early 1960's it was a vibrant and bustling place with all the factories, full of life and character. Today, despite the abundance of modern buildings the area seems to have lost its character. The streets, previously awash with families sitting on the walls outside their houses chatting and laughing and their children playing all manner of street games, are now strangely silent. Compared to how it was then it now seems quite deserted whenever I visit, except for some inconsiderate houses playing very loud pop music out of their open windows, which is surely very annoying to the neighbours. Still, I am sure that in the fullness of time the area will develop a character all of it's own again. West Silvertown was an island set between the Canning Town and Silvertown viaducts and the residents from the early 1900's shared a unique experience through two World Wars to the early 1960's when the Victorian terraced houses were finally demolished, so the camaraderie that I recall had developed over a considerable number of years.

33

The 2002 'friendsreunited' Reunion

In April 2002 Christine Sloan, who had lived at 6 Eastwood Road, and I arranged a reunion through contacts at the 'friendsreunited' Internet web site. About forty adults who had attended West Silvertown Primary School during the 1940/50 periods turned up at Lyle Park. Quite unbelievably, we were almost the only people in Lyle Park during that afternoon.

We all stood out like a sore thumb in the deserted Lyle Park that Sunday afternoon. We were a huge crowd, but in the 1950's we would just have blended in with the masses of people and activities that generally took place in the park on a busy Sunday afternoon. It was great seeing all those faces again after over forty years, some of which were immediately recognisable and others you would never have guessed who they were in a month of Sundays. It was also surprising how many of us had died during the course of the last five years. One thing is for sure; we all had an affinity with each other. Growing up in the West Silvertown hamlet during the 1940's and 1950's we shared certain values and there was a bond between us.

In 2003 I was speaking to one ex West Silvertown resident, Cissy Pattison who is now approaching her eighties. Cissy lived at 21 Westwood Road and in 1961 was re-housed in Canning Town. She told me that a few years ago she had a regular caller from the Newham Council and that one day, completely out of the blue, he asked her if she originally came from West Silvertown. She confirmed that she did and asked him how he knew. He replied that it is just that there is something in the character of West Silvertown people that shines through. Cissy's son Glen, who now lives in Upminster, still returns at least once a week just to sit down in Lyle Park, endeavouring to rekindle the magic of our lost childhood and the unique experiences we all shared having lived through that wonderful period in time. I certainly know the feeling, Glen!

The sad thing is that on the last few occasions that Joan and I have visited Lyle Park, during the last six months, we have been the only people in the entire park. We've sat on the seats at the very top of the park overlooking the Thames, where it's a real suntrap, bathed in sunshine and wondering where every one is while we tuck into our picnic. Without a shadow of doubt my quality of life and financial position are far in excess of what I could ever have imagined back in those 1950's schoolboy days. Yet, if it were at all possible would I choose to go back to the Silvertown slums, those poor utility days and live it all again, not changing a single thing? You bet I would! Only the second time around I would pay more attention to even the most insignificant of events, etching them on my mind so that I could recall them all with even greater clarity today.

34

Conned out of a car and the cancelled flight.

My life seems to have been filled with small insignificant coincidences, almost to the point that I felt at times that I was following some sort of predetermined and unchangeable script. It almost makes you believe in Guardian Angels. One single event was particularly significant. We found the early years of our marriage very difficult financially. We had our baby when I was nineteen years of age and struggling on a 'rate for age' wage. Even Stan Yates, the STC Personnel Manager who was aware of my low wage, asked how on Earth we would cope with the huge increase in rent for our new Basildon Council house. In January 1966 I attained 21 years of age and finally got the 'full adult' wage. We could never afford lavish holidays and I had always listened with envy to work colleagues after they returned from their Spanish package holidays stating how lovely the weather was, what great beaches and crystal clear water they had in Spain, what a great time they all had and how very cheap the cost of living was over there.

I thought that as a special treat, on now having a full adult wage, I would surprise Joan with a Spanish holiday. I went for the cheapest holiday there was which was with Lyons Tours flying out of Manston

Airport in Kent. It cost £67.00 for us both to have an 11-day all in package holiday at the Hotel Acapulco in Calella, on Spain's Costa Dorada. We flew out of Manston Airport on the first Saturday in June 1966 and had our holiday of a lifetime. Our daughter Joanne had striking blonde hair and was always made a great fuss of by the dark haired Spaniards. None of them spoke English like they do today therefore we could not understand a word they said, nevertheless we still made a lot of Spanish friends.

As 'Southerners' we were certainly in a minority with the other eighty odd holidaymakers, most of whom were Northerners, Lyons Tours being a North of England tour company. We got on really great with this bunch of Northerners they were very loud, but terrific fun to be with especially in the bar at night. We all had such a wonderful time that we made a pact that we would all return to the Hotel Acapulco the very first week in June next year, with Lyons Tours again. I also made a promise to the friendly hotel staff, via the Spanish-speaking courier of course, that I would return next year speaking their language. That last night at the resort, sitting in the open-air hotel bar was a really great finale to our first foreign holiday. As it was such a struggle for us to afford it in the first place I had just run out of spending money the day before. Fortunately, Tom, one of the kindly Northerners said, 'I don't want to take any of this foreign money home, so the drinks are on me!' He stuck the rest of his wad behind the bar and we all sat in one large group, with me still adamant that I would learn the language for next year and others stating that it was just the drink speaking and taking advanced bets that I wouldn't. As the coach turned up at about 1.00am I went to say goodbye to the female barmaid, who had during the course of the holiday taught me a few Spanish phrases. I called the Courier over and asked her to tell Isabella that next year I will definitely return to the Hotel and speak to her in her own language. Isabella just smiled, and said to the courier, 'Si, en sus suenos!' The Courier smiled back, nodded to Isabella and translated for me. She just said, 'In your dreams!' I looked back at Isabella, smiled and said, 'She doesn't know how determined I am!'

I bought a Spanish language course, with books and long play vinyl records, and I then listened to Spanish radio broadcasts from June to October 1966. I studied Spanish as soon as I got up each morning, then during both tea and lunch breaks in work and finally another hour's study when I arrived home in the evening. I was determined to live up to my promise by speaking the language when we all met up again the following June.

I still only had the Carlton Franco Suise bicycle in 1966 and cycled everywhere. I was anxious to ensure that I got the Lyons Tours brochure the moment it appeared in the travel agents to ensure I got an early booking to comply with the pact we had all made. I was also very keen to show off my Spanish speaking abilities to the rest of the group. Someone told me that the Lyons Brochure was in at Basildon Exchange Travel Agents. I knew a couple of our Standard Telephones local drivers and asked if one of them could pick up a Lyons brochure from the travel agent that very morning. By just before my lunch break I had filled in the booking form. We would fly out again from Manston Airport on Saturday 3rd June 1967. I couldn't wait to get to the travel agents to book the holiday. I had already 'phoned them and tried to get them to reserve it for me, promising to be down within an hour with the deposit, but they wouldn't.

I pedalled as fast as I could for the 2½-mile bike ride to Basildon Town Centre. Then, when I hit the huge central Basildon Town Centre roundabout something happened. The bike just would not go round the roundabout. A voice in my head was telling me to go home and let Joan know that I was booking the holiday. It was almost as if someone had hold of the handlebars. This was crazy, as I was in a rush anyway! I never consulted Joan over finances, ever! I went round the huge roundabout twice before I conceded and pedalling even faster headed for home. I reckoned that I didn't even have time enough to go into our house, so I just threw my bike on the front lawn and opened our letterbox. Looking down the hallway I saw Joan in the kitchen and shouted through the letterbox "Joan, I'm off to book the holiday." I immediately felt better, as if a weight had been taken off my mind and picked up my bike and started to cycle away. Joan opened the front door and called me back. I shouted back that I hadn't got the time. Joan shouted that it was important, so I cycled back to the house. Joan asked me to come into the house. I thought that maybe someone had died and it crossed my mind that would be a good excuse for being back to work late, but after I had booked the holiday.

Joan got me into the kitchen and started to tell me about a neighbour, living about four doors along the road, who got cars cheap, HP repossessions, she said. I couldn't believe it, here I was on a mission, having studied Spanish hours each day for nearly five months, and Joan was twittering on about someone who sold cheap cars. We argued for ages. Joan's point was that a Spanish holiday lasts for 10 days, but a car lasts all year. We could be independent and go where we wanted and when we wanted each weekend, she said. I was so desperate for this Spanish holiday I even said perhaps we could afford both, but really that was out of the question and I knew in my heart of hearts that Joan was right. I was just being selfish, so I said that I would speak to the neighbour that night. After speaking to him I agreed to buy a car from him and immediately start taking driving lessons.

My heart sunk when I finally tore up the booking form. I was so very disappointed that after all that intensive study of the Spanish language I was now denied the opportunity to put it into practice. Frequently, it went through my mind that if only I hadn't listened to that stupid voice in my head and cycled home that day then we would definitely be off on the Spanish holiday. Had I actually laid the non-returnable booking deposit we would have been completely committed to the holiday, as we certainly could not have afforded to lose all that hard earned cash.

As we did not have any savings we could not afford to buy the car outright, so we went to a finance company in Romford to borrow £380 for the car. That was a lot of money in those days. Also, I started taking driving lessons twice a week and was doing so well that my driving instructor advised me to put in for my driving test right away. Then, just days before Christmas 1966, we discovered that the neighbour was running a stolen car racket and we had lost everything. We were devastated, as we now owed a finance company £380, plus interest, for a car that we never had and all this just before Christmas. Even worse, as I had got in on a cancellation my driving test was the day after we discovered our unfortunate predicament. My heart was not in it and I failed the driving test. I cursed our bad luck, feeling that life had just dealt me a very cruel hand! Joan said it would be a good idea if we sent 2½-year old Joanne to a child minder and she went out to find some work to help us pay off the debt. Cash-strapped, we went back to West

Silvertown for Christmas and stayed with my parents in Parker Street. After hearing our story Joan's dad generously offered to loan us the money to pay off the finance company, but I would not hear of it. I told him that was our lesson in life – the alarm bells were there ringing all the time, but I just wouldn't listen to them. Enough people warned us that the deal we were getting was almost too good to be true but I was so focused on what I felt I had to do that I just did not listen.

The following year we were sitting in doors watching the television when I picked up the newspaper to see what else was on later in the evening. Looking at the date I noticed it was Saturday 3rd June. I said to Joan, "Do you know where we would be now if you had kept your mouth shut?" Joan looked puzzled. "No", she said, "What do you mean?" I replied, "I mean that by now we would be well on our way to Manston Airport." Joan drew in her breath, sighed and nodded her head towards me, as if she were to blame. I felt rotten and said, "No, its not your fault love, I shouldn't have kept on going around the roundabout." I teased her all evening. "They are all looking at the airport doors now, for us!" I said, "They are just about to take off now." I did feel I had broken the pact and let them all down and cursed my dithering on the roundabout last October. I said to Joan, "I do envy them, I bet Tom is looking round the cabin now expecting us to burst through the doors at any moment." I finally shook my head and said to Joan "I've let us all down, lets forget it now."

That was the end of the banter and we sat there watching the TV until around 11 O' clock, when we mutually agreed that it was time for bed. As I got up to turn off the TV I still vividly recall being frozen in my steps halfway across the lounge when a large 'NEWSFLASH' appeared on the screen. The announcer said that there had been reports of an air crash. A British charter flight had crashed into the Pyrenees. I looked at Joan and shook my head, "No chance" I said, "There are thousands of flights every night, it's not our one."

In Monday's newspapers we read the full story. Yes, it was our Manston Airport flight to Barcelona. The Invicta Airways (Air Ferry Ltd) DC4 turbo-prop aeroplane had crashed into the foot of the Pyranees killing 83 holidaymakers and five-cabin crew. There were no survivors and on reading the list of the dead we recognised many of the names from last years holiday. I was quite astounded by this terrible event and my mind went back to the struggle I had with my bicycle on the roundabout, with this voice in my head that kept telling me to cycle home and tell Joan about booking the holiday. That voice had saved our lives. Come to think of it, that voice did sound very much like the same voice that made me sit downstairs on the bus, opposite that miserable girl, all those years ago in Silvertown.

Printed in the United Kingdom
by Lightning Source UK Ltd.
133017UK00002B/65/P